# THE Handcrafted WEDDING

More Than **300** Fun and Imaginative
Handcrafted Ways to Personalize
Your Wedding Day

EMMA ARENDOSKI

SELLERS
PUBLISHING

## Published by Sellers Publishing, Inc.

Copyright © 2012 Sellers Publishing, Inc.
Text © 2012 Emma Arendoski
All rights reserved.

Photography and resource credits appear on page 172.

Sellers Publishing, Inc.
161 John Roberts Road, South Portland, Maine 04106
Visit our Web site: www.sellerspublishing.com
E-mail: rsp@rsvp.com

ISBN: 13: 978-1-4162-0666-8
e-ISBN: 978-1-4162-0860-0
Library of Congress Control Number: 2012931602

10 9 8 7 6 5 4 3 2 1

Printed and bound in China.

# Dedication

―◦―

*This book is dedicated to Andrew, my husband and best friend.*
*Thank you for your endless love, support, and encouragement.*
*I am the luckiest girl in the world. I love you!*

*Thank you to Mom and Dad for giving me roots, wings, and faith. I love you both.*

*Thank you to my family and friends for your encouragement and support.*
*I feel incredibly blessed to be surrounded by such amazing people.*

# CONTENTS

# Introduction

In your mind's eye, does your perfect wedding day include charming, handcrafted details, delightful DIY (do-it-yourself) ideas, and a style all your own? If so, you've come to the right place.

My name is Emma and I eat, sleep, and blog about weddings. While most brides stop obsessing over wedding details and flipping through magazines postnuptials, my love for weddings stuck around for good. I was done planning my wedding and yet I continued to seek the most inspirational, creative ideas for weddings. I knew then that I had found my true passion in life.

I am the founder and editor-in-chief of EmmalineBride.com, a unique wedding blog with a primary focus on handcrafted weddings. I've often been asked, why handcrafted weddings? Handcrafted weddings are personal, heartfelt, and creative. No two couples share the same story, so why should two weddings share the same details? After my sweetheart proposed, I did what most brides do: I went shopping. I suppose I expected wedding inspiration to leap off the shelves, but unfortunately nothing spoke to me personally. The biggest day of one's life ought to be special and unique . . . I knew there had to be a better way.

In just a few searches online, I was able to toss out my wedding-planning playbook and start from scratch. In doing so, I changed my perception of wedding planning — and my life — forever. I discovered an incredible number of artisans online who handcrafted wedding-day details — such as ring pillows, veils, gowns, centerpieces, and more — from their own home (not some factory). Each item is made with love, care, and two hands, with each individual item unlike any other. I knew there had to be other brides like me who would benefit from a place that would share handmade wedding details and give artisans an opportunity to shine. Emmaline Bride became that place. I wholeheartedly love handmade weddings and continue to be inspired on a daily basis.

I wrote *The Handcrafted Wedding* to kick-start your wedding-planning experience and inspire you to think outside the box. You will find yourself crafting DIY ideas, using innovative wedding approaches, and learning new twists to the traditional planning experience. Your labor of love will result in a memorable wedding day, one that guests will be talking about long after the day is through.

How will your love story be remembered?

—E.

P.S. Visit EmmalineBride.com and click on Book for tips on where to buy DIY supplies and handmade items.

# CHAPTER 1

# You're Engaged!

He popped the questions and you said yes — now what's next? One of the first tasks on your new to-do list is to spread the exciting news: you're getting married!

But before you even do that, consider whether you'd like your wedding to have a theme. If you would, you might want that in place first, so everything related to your wedding integrates your vision.

# Picking a Wedding Theme

There are no boundaries and no limits when it comes to selecting a theme for your wedding. Here are some ideas to get you started.

## • SEASONS •

Seasons can provide plenty of inspiration, from color schemes to flowers. If a particular season plays a significant role in your love story, consider setting the date during those months, with thematic elements worked into your wedding planning.

Which season tells your love story best?

### Winter

A winter wedding combines the good tidings of the holidays with the togetherness of friends and family. An indoor ceremony can be decorated en masse with green wreaths and an abundance of holly, complete with candlelit lanterns to illuminate the aisleway. Hang mistletoe over the entrance to your reception hall, and greet guests with a roaring fire and a glass of eggnog.

Or go with an icy-blue color palette, using metallics to adorn the reception hall and ceremony seating. Piano music can serenade guests during dinner and, depending upon the climate of your location, your guests can enjoy the romance of a snow-covered landscape from the inviting warmth of the ballroom.

## *Spring*

Spring says sunshine, the light scent of blossoms in the air, and birds chirping as you arrive at the ceremony. Bridesmaids dressed in the bright colors of the season walk down the aisle carrying bouquets of tulips, while the flower girl holds a basket full of daisies. Outdoor greenery provides a beautiful backdrop for wedding photographs, while guests arriving at the reception site enjoy freshly squeezed lemonade and light hors d'oeuvres before dinner is served.

## *Summer*

A handcrafted summer wedding can be a backyard ceremony, where you walk down the aisle accompanied by your favorite song played on acoustic guitar. Bridesmaids are dressed in airy sundresses, carrying wildflower bouquets. Following the ceremony, guests enjoy a cocktail hour and engage in low-impact outdoor activities (such as horseshoes or a beanbag toss) as they await a catered dinner in a tented reception site. By night, lanterns create an illuminated dance floor, and guests enjoy a bonfire with a do-it-yourself s'mores station.

## Fall

If you love nature, a handcrafted wedding in the fall may be perfect for you. A woodland-inspired wedding — complete with a ceremony in the woods, with straw bales for guests to sit on — may be nontraditional, but offers abundant beauty courtesy of Mother Nature. Guests don't notice the chill in the air, when there's a basket of cozy blankets and throws to borrow and a coffee bar at the reception, complete with chocolate chip cookies ready for dunking. Another option is a ceremony held in your favorite park (one that is available to rent), followed by a reception indoors. That way you can combine the beauty of an autumnal afternoon with the warmth and coziness of an indoor reception.

## • HOBBIES AND INTERESTS •

When you met, was there a particular hobby you had in common? Do you spend weekends riding bicycles, attending concerts, or browsing the shelves at a local bookstore? How the two of you spend free time together can be used to create a wedding theme.

### Cooking

A couple that cooks together may want a kitchen-related theme. Plan a wedding reception catered by a favorite restaurant, with a menu of your favorite entrees. On your invitation's reply card, include an area for guests to select a preferred dessert option, like "Cake" or "Pie." For favors, bake homemade sugar cookies and buy cookie cutters with your initials; send them home with guests in hand-decorated paper bags. Create a fabric banner using iron-on letters (available at craft stores) to spell out "Love Is Sweet." Instead of a traditional wedding cake, offer guests a dessert buffet with macaroons and other cookies, pastries, and pies. Sounds sweet to me!

### Outdoor Activities

Nature-loving couples can create a wedding with an outdoorsy theme. For instance, you could kick off a bicycle-themed wedding by using the image of a bicycle built for two on all your wedding correspondence.

For wedding favors, wrap granola bars with a custom label (printed from your computer). For the bar, serve a bicycle-themed craft beer like New Belgium Brewing Company's Fat Tire beer. Fill woven bicycle baskets with flowers to use as table centerpieces, and make the cake topper a pair of his-and-her bicycles. Put "Just" and "Married" signs on the backs of your bikes and take a quick postwedding bicycle ride — dress, tuxedo, and all.

Other activities, such as hiking, canoeing, mountain climbing, and camping, can provide tons of wedding inspiration. Include a do-it-yourself trail-mix station, complete with small decorative bags for guests to fill as favors. A personalized cake topper with a couple, campfire, and tent would incorporate a camping theme perfectly. Utilize unexpected elements throughout your décor. A friend who loves to kayak decided to have her guests sign an oar instead of using a traditional guest book. Afterwards, she gave the oar a coating of clear wood sealant to preserve the signatures, and it's now displayed in her home.

### Boating

Imagine bridesmaids and groomsmen dressed in navy blue, with ivory rope bracelets for the ladies (you can find these at www.junghwa.etsy.com) and rope boutonnières for the men. Create table centerpieces with glass hurricane lamps filled with sand or seashells and a candle; blue-and-white-striped table runners complete the look. Continue the theme on the menu with shrimp cocktail and lobster bisque. For favors, consider lobster-shaped lollipops (check out Sugar Bellys Boutique on Etsy.com), sailboat-shaped cookies, or shell-shaped soaps packed in muslin favor bags stamped with anchors.

### Birding

Wedding invitations with a pair of birds sitting in a tree (probably k-i-s-s-i-n-g) kickstart this themed wedding. Offer miniature toss bags of birdseed for guests to throw as you proceed down the aisle (if your wedding is outdoors), use a white birdcage to house wedding cards at the reception, and place a pair of custom lovebirds on your cake as a topper. Gift guests with birdseed favors (you can find them at www.naturefavors.com). For centerpieces, create bird-themed vignettes with faux bird nests (found at craft stores) filled with Jordan almonds (as the "eggs").

### Reading

If you love to browse bookstores with your honey, or if you stole a kiss while studying in the college library, or you both always have your noses in a novel, a book-themed wedding could be a perfect choice. Classic hardcover books, table numbers crafted from library cards, and bookmark favors for guests are just a few thematic ideas for bookworms. Create a photo booth with books and reading glasses as props. For an easy-to-DIY guest book, purchase a blank scrapbook album and glue library due-date card pockets throughout the book. On your guest-book table, include a sign asking to "Borrow a minute of their time," and instruct guests to take a blank due-date card, sign it, add a message, and stamp the date. (You can purchase blank cards and pockets at Amazon.com or from a school-supply store.) A cake topper with a stack of books ties it all together.

### The Movies

If movies are your passion and you can recite lines from your favorites, verbatim, or spent your first date holding hands at the local cinema, then movie themes may be just the one for you. Send a movie-themed save the date made to look like a ticket, name each reception table after a favorite movie, and set up a popcorn-and-candy buffet table for guests to enjoy after dinner is served. Wrap up boxes of candy for guests to take home as favors, and make your entrance as husband and wife at the reception a red-carpet affair.

### Make It Country

If you'd rather wear a pair of cowboy boots than heels, consider a country theme for your wedding. For example, serve lemonade or iced tea in Mason jars, tie the knot in a barn (decorated for the occasion), or rent a dude ranch for your wedding reception. Wear your cowboy boots, carry a bouquet of wildflowers down the aisle, and offer guests favors of miniature apple pies in bakery boxes tied up with twine.

### On the Beach

Go barefoot and get married at the seashore, or bring the party indoors with a beach wedding theme. Serve up a menu of seafood, create table tableaux with starfish and sea glass, and send guests home with gift bags of seashells.

Try this idea on for size: purchase flip-flops (Old Navy sells them for around $2.50 a pair) in a variety of sizes. Put them in a bushel basket with a sign for guests to "Pick a Pair," kick off their heels, and dance in a more comfortable pair of shoes.

### A Very Caffeinated Wedding

If you met in a café or you and your honey adore coffee, consider this theme. Partially fill small centerpiece vases with coffee beans, then place flowers or a candle on top. For favors, send guests home with individual-serving packets of your favorite flavored coffees (Target sells them for about a dollar each). You can also order custom favor bags of gourmet coffee beans from www.aproposroasters.com. Create a coffee bar with different flavors of coffee, toppings, and whipped cream. Don't forget donuts for dunking!

For a bridal-party gift they'll reuse for years, buy ceramic coffee mugs in white. Use a specialty marker (like Pébéo Porcelaine 150 china paint markers) to write each attendant's name on the mug, or you can stencil their names. The marker dries after 24 hours; then bake the mug in the oven as directed for an enamel finish.

### Sports

Did he pop the question at a baseball game? Do you play on the same softball team every year? For a baseball-themed wedding, you can design your save-the-date cards to look like trading cards. Instead of having friends and family sign a guest book, have them sign baseballs you've left out for that purpose, along with permanent markers. Carry the theme over to your menu and serve stadium fare, like hot dogs and peanuts, during the cocktail hour.

## Engagement and Save-the-Date Announcements

Once you've selected a theme and set the date, it's time to tell the world: "I'm getting married!" You can do this with an engagement announcement or a save the date.

An engagement announcement can be printed on card stock and mailed to family and friends. It tells guests the news without setting an official wedding date. To make your announcement even more memorable, share how he popped the question: for example, "He surprised me with cider, donuts, and a gorgeous diamond ring at the cider mill. I said yes!" Your loved ones will be delighted to hear how it happened.

A save the date includes the wedding date and general location; no need to give specifics yet. It is typically sent six to eight months before the wedding. If you send it any earlier than that, your guest list may not be finalized yet; if you send it too late, it defeats the purpose. A save the date is not mandatory, but it is a fun way to share the news of your upcoming nuptials with guests in a more personal manner. If you are planning a destination wedding, a save the date is strongly recommended to give guests plenty of time to make travel arrangements.

### Postcard Save the Date

This is a popular choice for couples; it requires less postage and does not need an envelope. A photograph is key to a memorable save-the-date postcard. Enlist the assistance of a photographer to capture you and your fiancé in your element: on bikes, tossing around a football, visiting the local zoo. A handmade prop such as a banner can add a personalized touch to your photo. Use iron-on transfer numbers to announce the date of the wedding. You can also stencil or sponge paint them on. You and your fiancé can then hold up the banner in your photo.

Once you've selected your photograph, find a printing service online to create the perfect postcard, like www.MagnetStreet.com, which offers wedding-specific templates. Upload your photo, input your text and wedding date, and you're done.

Most print shops — both online and locally — offer magnetic paper as a printing option, which can turn your save the date into a fun refrigerator magnet. If you decide to take advantage of this, you can't just put stamps on magnets and pop them in the mail; they'll need to be sent in individual envelopes.

### Pencil-It-In Save the Date

Before cell phones had calendars, people scheduled a date the old-fashioned way, by "penciling it in" their date book. Have no. 2 pencils custom printed with your names and the wedding date. Or, you can make your own, using a fine-tip marker to write the information on the pencils. Be sure to write it near the eraser end, as the message will wear off when the pencils are sharpened. Then, print tags that read, "Pencil In the Date!" Punch a hole through each tag, run twine through it, and tie tightly around two pencils.

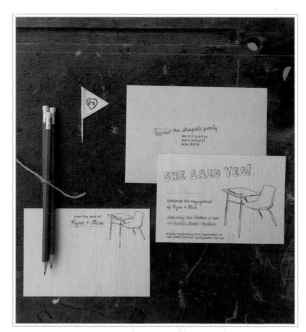

Send them off to guests in padded envelopes, so the pencils don't break in the mail.

### *"Borrow" the Date*

If you're planning a book-themed wedding, you can turn an ordinary library card into a save-the-date bookmark. Punch a hole at the top of the card, tie a ribbon through it, and stamp your names, the date, and the location onto the card. One of my favorite save-the-date ideas is from Akimbo Design (www.akimbo.com.au). It features a library due-date card, pocket, and vintage-style stamp with the wedding date. The save the date asks guests, ever so sweetly, "May we borrow you?"

### *Blooming Save the Date*

Wouldn't it be lovely to know that little garden patches of wildflowers, vegetables, and herbs were springing up in your honor? A seed packet save the date can do just that, tying into a garden wedding theme or simply showing your love for gardening. Stamp the outside of a small, muslin drawstring bag (or spice bag) with a pretty floral stamp, wedding monogram, or the date of your wedding. Fill the bag with your favorite wildflower, vegetable, or herb seeds, wrap a ribbon around the bag, and attach a small, printed-from-home tag with a message, such as:

> *Plant these seeds and water, too;*
> *When they bloom, we'll say, I do.*

Guests can either plant the seeds in their backyard or in a planter to await the arrival of your wedding day.

# The Invitation

The wedding invitation isn't just a fancy card and stamped envelope. To ensure that your invitation stands out, you can include a few fanciful details. For instance, instead of printing address labels from a computer, handwrite them. Your guests are hand selected, so a handwritten envelope makes it feel more personal. If you lack pretty penmanship (or patience), hire a calligrapher to help.

Another way to add a personal touch is with a custom postage stamp of you and your fiancé. Companies like www.Stamps.com will print postage stamps using a photo you upload from your home computer; the best part is that they don't cost any more than regular postage stamps.

Wedding invitations are typically sent out six to eight weeks before the wedding. Remember, though, that if you are having them professionally printed, you may need to order well in advance. Most printers will give you a timeline for wedding invitations — just ask.

## • FORMAL OR INFORMAL? •

The wedding invitation is a reflection of the formality of your wedding. For a sit-down dinner reception select a formal invitation, for a more casual affair, almost anything can work. The invitation (like all wedding-day correspondence) can be helpful in setting the tone and theme of your wedding, so be sure it follows suit appropriately.

Wedding invitations often include an array of information: the invitation, a response card (accompanied by a self-addressed, stamped envelope), directions to the ceremony or reception, rehearsal dinner invitation, etc. Do something different with your invitation. Give guests a sneak peek into the fun party that awaits them by sharing the delicious menu you have created, highlight local hot spots they can enjoy while they are in town, and suggest choices for accommodations.

A handcrafted wedding boasts many beautifully planned details, and the invitations kick those other invitations' *you-know-what* nearly every time. Here are some of my favorite ideas.

### Vintage-Handkerchief Invitations

A fun informal invitation can be made using vintage handkerchiefs. They often feature unusual patterns or prints, and hand-drawn or hand-embroidered monograms. Why not use them to print the details of your wedding and go paper free, as creatively imagined by the team at Paper and Thread (www. paperandthread.com)? Each handkerchief is hand selected and unique, so no two guests will receive the same one.

Or, for a personal, handmade gift for your bridal party, embroider a handkerchief with their initials or a wedding-related design and wrap it around his or her invitation.

### Wooden Invitations

Can you imagine a wedding invitation printed on wood? The design folks at Night Owl Paper Goods (www.nightowlpapergoods.com) have created a unique alternative for couples when paper just won't do. These invitations are custom made and stamped onto wood grain for a frame-worthy wedding invitation you'll cherish — and guests will love to receive!

## Ode to the Classics

If you love classic literature, consider using your favorite book or play as the theme for your wedding. For instance, this delightful variation (at left) on a formal wedding invitation — cleverly designed by Akimbo Design — captures *A Midsummer Night's Dream* in an ethereal, romantic way. The invitation is even printed on birch to give it a rustic texture.

## Sweeter Details

Design your own invitations! Visit a store like Michael's or Target that offers blank wedding invitations in a box with instructions on how to print them. Use your computer and the included templates to print invitations at home, or bring your design to a local print shop.

To dress up a simple invitation, add embellishments. For a natural touch, adorn invitations with raffia, burlap, or natural twine.

If you love vintage details, wrap each invitation in a paper doily and tie a bow around it with a length of narrow ribbon. For added texture, use fabric doilies; for a pop of color, dye the doilies in a favorite shade.

You can also use a craft-paper punch to add edging details — like eyelets — around the border of each invitation.

## CHAPTER 2
# The Bride and Groom

——◄○►——

Deciding what to wear for your wedding day should be fun and exciting. Don't fall into the mind-set that you must dress a certain way because tradition says so. The handcrafted wedding is all about being yourself, so wear whatever makes you happy. This means the groom doesn't have to wear a tuxedo. Heck, he doesn't even have to wear a suit. Brides can dive into the tulle pool with a whole lot of poof, or opt for something simple like a sundress. If it makes you happy, wear it. The only thing you're required to wear on your wedding day is a smile.

The handcrafted wedding is about incorporating your own personal style into all aspects of the day, including the clothing. I'll show you how to add unique, handcrafted touches to your wedding wardrobe and provide a few tips on attire you may not have considered, beginning with The Bride.

# The Bride

The bridal dress is one of the most beautiful details of the wedding day. Once you've found The One to marry, it's time to find the perfect dress.

Since *The Handcrafted Wedding* focuses on making unforgettable memories along the way, be sure to bring someone special with you while shopping for dresses, like your mom or best friend.

Before shopping with my mom, I asked her what her wedding gown looked like. Instead of telling me, she showed it to me, packed away in a huge box in the basement — it was a gorgeous, floor-length taffeta wedding gown with lacy sleeves, a lace neckline, and hand-sewn embellishments. Naturally, I didn't waste a minute before putting it on and wearing it around the house, a memory I'll cherish forever.

Most brides want to pick out their own wedding gown, but that doesn't mean your wedding gown won't be useful to a future daughter or niece. Holding onto your dress not only provides you with a lovely keepsake, it can also be the source of plenty of *something old* or *something borrowed* ideas to pass along to future brides. For instance, I love the idea of taking a piece of fabric, lace, or tulle from your mother's or grandmother's gown and fashioning it into a dress sash, a small flower brooch pin, or a hair accessory to wear on your own wedding day.

## • THE WEDDING DRESS •

Here are a few of my favorite ideas for making a wedding dress uniquely your own.

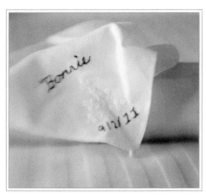

### Handkerchief

Your mother's wedding-day handkerchief can be wrapped and pinned around your bouquet as a decorative handle, or it can be sewn underneath the bottom layer of your gown.

### Hem

Ask a seamstress to stitch "something blue" into your gown with a sweet and subtle blue thread added to the hem of your gown. Or embroider a blue heart, your monogram, or your initials onto a small embroidery square. Then bring it your seamstress and have her sew it into the hem.

### Buttons

If you love the look of round buttons — the classic elegance of a bridal gown with buttons running down the back — don't turn down a gown simply because it lacks them. Buttons are a customizable option that can be added to your gown with the help of a seamstress. If your gown has a zipper, have buttons added along the side.

### A Pocket

Why rely on a purse to carry your must-haves on your wedding day? Have your seamstress sew in a pocket if it won't interfere with the drape of the gown. You'll then have a convenient place to hold your vows, or a handkerchief for when you start to tear up, or a lipstick for touch-ups throughout the day.

### Sleeves

If you love the look of a particular gown but dislike the idea of going strapless, ask your seamstress to add sleeves. Delicate cap sleeves, short sleeves, or lacy long sleeves will make you more comfortable, and will give the gown your own personalized touch.

### Additional Length

Since I'm tall, everything I buy requires additional length. The same applied for my wedding gown, particularly since I was wearing heels.

If you are adding length to your gown, ask your seamstress if you can keep any remaining fabric after it has been hemmed. You can use the fabric to make a keepsake ring pillow.

### Heirloom Jewelry

If you have a piece of heirloom jewelry with delicate beads, pearls, or a gemstone, find out if it is possible to have a few of the beads or pearls sewn into your gown, or whether it's possible to incorporate the piece as an embellishment on a dress sash.

### Crinoline

Also known as a petticoat, a crinoline is a full-layer slip that goes under your gown. A crinoline gives your gown a fuller look, contributing to a gown's "twirlability" on the dance floor. I love a crinoline because you barely notice you are wearing it, yet it has a huge effect on the flow of your gown. If you crave plenty of gown volume, you'll love it.

If you're planning on wearing a crinoline, think about this: a dyed crinoline. You can dye it any color of the rainbow, and it provides a colorful "peek" under your gown as you walk down the aisle. Need "something blue"? A soft, subtle, light-blue crinoline underneath your gown will do. You can also go bold with hot pink, turquoise, or yellow, as long as the gown itself is opaque enough that the color doesn't show through the fabric.

## Sash

To add a handcrafted touch to your gown without sewing into it, consider a dress sash, made of lace, fabric, or ribbon, which can be added to almost any gown. It can incorporate beading, rhinestones, crystals, floral pieces, vintage brooches — anything — with a simple pin backing and a dab of glue.

If you want to wear a vintage brooch for the ceremony as "something blue" but you don't want to pin it directly to your gown, pin it to a long piece of coordinating satin ribbon and wear it as a sash. Tulle is another option, and it is very inexpensive. A length of tulle — which comes in a wide range of colors — can be tied around your waist into a large bow in the back. This is a nice choice for bridesmaid dresses, too.

For an elegant dress sash you can make at home, buy silk, satin, or lace fabric. Cut it so it is 2 inches wide and 3 yards long. Use an iron to remove wrinkles. You can leave the sash plain or embellish it with a flower pin, fabric appliqué, or another favorite accessory. Wrap the fabric around your waist comfortably and tie a bow in the back. If the bow is larger than you'd like, trim it to your preferred length, turn under, and hem stitch.

For a sparkly sash, use seed beads, rhinestones, or crystals to embellish satin fabric. Cut 3 yards of satin 1 inch wide. Find the center of the sash, then lightly mark in pencil on either side of the center point, to indicate the area of the sash you want to fill with your adornments. Lay the fabric onto a flat surface and begin fastening adornments at one end of the area with a hot-glue gun, moving across the fabric a section at a time. Continue gluing until the entire surface area between your pencil lines is covered. The process may take an hour or two to complete. Once the glue is dry, shake the sash lightly to remove loose beads. Look for sparse areas, and fill them in with additional beads. When it's complete, cut the ends of the sash at an angle; tie it around your waist and secure it with a bow in the back.

For "something old" or "something borrowed," you can have a pocket square or handkerchief from your father or grandfather made into a fabric rosette and pinned to your sash.

## Dress Hanger

The perfect wedding dress deserves one final handcrafted touch: a dress hanger! Make your own with an ordinary wooden hanger, a metal stamping kit, a metal block, and a hammer. The hardened steel stamps make it easy to inscribe anything you wish onto your hanger, like "Mrs.," "Bride," or your wedding date. Place the wooden hanger on the metal block, hold it in place, and stamp your message onto the hanger by tapping each stamp with the hammer.

Another option is to order a personalized dress hanger (one source is www. myambercolouredworld.etsy.com, which features a wooden hanger and a metal piece fashioned to say "Mrs." with your new last name, or any sentiment you wish, as pictured below).

# • THE BAG •

You'll need to carry around plenty of things on your wedding day. If you don't have a pocket in your dress, you'll want to find a bridal bag you'll love to hold.

### Borrow It

My "something borrowed" was my mother's wedding purse. If your mother, grandmother, or favorite aunt has a purse you'd like to borrow, ask!

### Personalize It

Add an element of personalization to the clutch; for instance, purchase the same fabric used in your bridesmaid dresses to create a rosette to sew or pin onto your clutch. It is a nice, subtle way to coordinate with your girls.

If you like to embroider or do cross-stitch, stitch a tag and sew it into the inner lining of your clutch. It can include your monogram and wedding date. Iron-on transfers will make the work easier and are available at all craft stores.

If you have a brooch you'd like to make part of your wedding outfit but don't want to pin it to your dress, it can find a home on your bridal clutch. A vintage pin or an heirloom piece, no matter the provenance, is a striking addition. Thrift stores and estate sales are good sources.

### A Ribbon Handle

In lieu of a traditional clutch chain or handle, try something a bit more handcrafted, like ribbon. It will add a whimsical touch and can be tied into your wedding color palette. Just remove the chain or handle and tie a ribbon securely to either end, firmly knotted. Use heavy, high-quality ribbon that can withstand the wear and tear of the day.

## • THE GARTER •

The tossing of the garter is an old tradition that is said to bring luck to whomever catches it. Today, since garters are increasingly more of a keepsake than a wear-and-toss item, brides customarily buy two garters: one to keep and one to toss.

Traditionally, a garter is nothing more than an elasticized length of fabric finished with a ribbon bow — simple and sweet. There are unlimited possibilities for personalization, including crafting it from vintage fabric, having it embroidered with your monogram or a school emblem, or sewing on a tag that has your favorite quote or song lyrics stitched into or printed on it.

Your garter is also an easy place to incorporate "something blue." Have a small blue button or blue feather sewn onto your garter.

Garters aren't just for the bride, either. Consider gifting a handcrafted keepsake garter to each of your bridesmaids. Be sure to sew a sentimental tag inside, like "Thanks for being my bridesmaid!" or "Love you!" Add a small rosette in her favorite color to each garter. Be sure to snap a shot during the wedding with you all revealing your garters!

## • THE SHOES •

Put your personal stamp on the day by wearing your favorite kind of shoes, whether they be mile-high stilettos, flats, sandals, sneakers, or cowboy boots. If you don't normally wear heels, your wedding day is not the time to try out a pair. Your feet will be screaming before you even get down the aisle. Wear whatever makes your feet happy, and you'll be comfortable all day long.

Once you've selected the type of shoe, it's time to add a little handcrafted flair.

### Glitter Flats

Turn a plain pair of flats into sparkling shoes with glitter! Craft your own with silver or gold glitter, glue sealant (one that dries clear, like Mod Podge), a sponge brush, and clear acrylic sealant spray. Create a mix with the glue sealant and glitter, and apply it evenly to the shoes with a sponge brush. Once dry, apply a second (and third, if required) coat to fully cover the shoes. When completely dry, spray the shoes evenly with clear sealant. Let the shoes dry overnight before wearing them down the aisle.

### Sparkle Heels

Turn a plain pair of heels into wedding wear with rhinestones applied to the heels. Attach small (3mm) rhinestones (round, with a flat back) to the heels using a hot-glue gun. When complete, apply a coat of clear sealant spray so the rhinestones won't budge.

### Flip-Flops/Sandals

Beach-loving brides, why not wear sandals or flip-flops? Order a custom pair online from a place like www.sandalista.com, where you can upload a favorite photo or a custom design to be printed onto a new pair of flip-flops.

Getting married on the beach? Purchase a pair of flip-flops with words embossed on the bottom ("Bride" or "Mrs."), designed to leave an imprint in the sand.

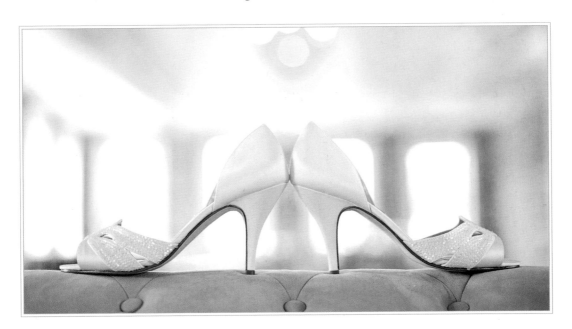

## Shoe Clips

This is a fun way to change the look of a pair of shoes instantly. Shoe clips are embellishments — rhinestones, feathers, fabric flowers, crystals, lace — secured to an alligator clip that you can add to or remove from a shoe with ease. Take a trip to the craft store, and select a favorite accoutrement and a pair of small alligator clips. Glue your adornment of choice to each of the clips. Then just clip them in place for the wedding day. Keep an eye out for vintage shoe clips, which were popular from the 1920s through the 1940s, in antique stores and consignment shops. Also, clip-on earrings can be used as shoe clips.

## Secret Soles

Here's something you can try. A few days before the wedding, ask each bridesmaid to sign her name on the bottom of your wedding shoes with a permanent marker. Allow the signatures to dry overnight. After the wedding is over, look at the bottoms of your shoes; supposedly whoever's name hasn't worn off completely will be the next one to get married.

## Last-Minute "Something Blue"

For a no-fuss "something blue," paint your toenails your favorite shade of blue.

## • THE VEIL AND OTHER HAIR ACCESSORIES •

No matter what new trend emerges in the wedding world, the veil is always a classic look — and for good reason. Veils are typically handcrafted and can feature lace, beads, rhinestones, crystals, and other beautiful embellishments that artisans spend hours sewing together, a single stitch at a time.

When searching for my wedding veil, I thought it would be fun to try on my mom's, which was sitting in a box in the basement. Who knew I'd fall in love with it? My mom's veil — my "something old" — was everything I wanted: not too long, not too short, with just the right amount of volume. My mother updated it by crafting a new hair comb for me. I also used her bridal purse, which was a gift given to her on her wedding day by my grandmother, as my "something borrowed."

### Birdcage Veil

A birdcage veil — made popular in the 1920s and still glamorous today — is worn on one side of the bride's head and covers a minimal portion of her eyes. More of a fashion statement than a veil, it can be comfortably worn with any hairstyle. To turn an ordinary birdcage veil into an extraordinary one, dye the tulle in your favorite color. I've seen brides with these veils in cream, yellow, gray, black, hot pink, green, and "something blue."

If you have an heirloom or vintage veil, but it isn't exactly your style, consider turning it into a birdcage veil by attaching a piece of it to a pretty comb.

## Feather Hair Comb

Feathers are a beautiful and unexpected alternative to a bridal veil and can incorporate a favorite color, "something blue," or traditional bridal ivory or white. You can attach them to a hair comb for an easy embellishment of any wedding hairstyle. You can also craft them for your bridesmaids. For even more fun, throw a party and craft them together, supplying all the necessary crafting gear (feathers, hot-glue guns, alligator clips, beads, rhinestones, crystals, ribbons). Have each bridesmaid make her own to wear on the wedding day, a gift she'll be sure to cherish.

## "Something Blue" Barrette

A simple "something blue" can be crafted by adding a blue rhinestone, feather, or rosette to a barrette. Glue your blue embellishment to a small piece of felt and attach it to the barrette with hot glue.

## Pearl Hair Comb

Embellish a standard hair comb with pearls. Take a hair comb (approximately 7cm long) in your hair color, and cut a satin ribbon to match its length. Glue the ribbon to the top of the comb with hot glue, then cover the surface of the ribbon with flat-back pearl beads (4mm), also attaching them with hot glue. Let it dry completely before wearing it.

**A floral headband** is a great alternative for the bride to wear on the wedding day in lieu of a traditional veil. They also make nice handcrafted gifts for the bridesmaids.

## For this project, you'll need the following supplies for each headband:

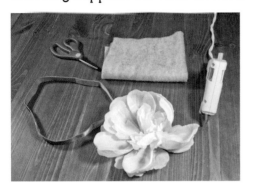

- **fabric scissors**
- **silk flower** (large bloom preferred)
- **hot-glue gun**
- **felt** (in a neutral tone)
- **elastic** (For mine, I purchased the 4 pack stretch headband set in pink, by Julie Comstock (http://laliberi.eksuccessbrands.com/dept/Julie+Comstock.aspx); if you can't find an elastic band in a color you love, buy a white elastic band, sold at craft stores near the sewing supplies.)
- **soft measuring tape, white thread, and needle if using white elastic band**

Before you begin, cut the stem off the silk flower so you have a flat bottom. If this causes the flower to fall apart, use small dabs of the glue to reattach the petals. If you are not using a presewn elastic band, use the tape to measure your head around the area where you will wear the headband. Cut the elastic to that length and sew the ends together.

1. Cut out two circles from the felt, large enough to cover the bottom of the bloom but not so big that they are visible.

2. Use dabs of glue to attach one felt circle to the bottom of the flower where you cut the stem off. Press firmly.

3. Then, place one or two dabs of glue in the middle of the elastic. Center it across the bloom on top of the felt piece and press firmly.

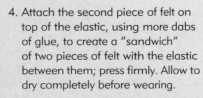

4. Attach the second piece of felt on top of the elastic, using more dabs of glue, to create a "sandwich" of two pieces of felt with the elastic between them; press firmly. Allow to dry completely before wearing.

## • BRIDAL JEWELRY •

Jewelry can add both style and sentiment to your wedding day. Once you've decided which style of jewelry you'd like to wear, find a way to incorporate sentiment. For instance, ask a family member if you may borrow a strand of pearls or earrings. Or wear a locket necklace with a picture of a loved one, or a cherished necklace your fiancé bought you during your courtship.

One of my own personal touches was my wedding band. My husband and I both opted for simple white-gold bands and had them engraved. We have a favorite song with two lines that mean a great deal to us — they express how we felt about our love when it began and how we will always remember to keep that feeling alive. One line is engraved inside by husband's band, the other in mine.

If a song isn't something you share in common, consider engraving the wedding date, your initials, a short quote, or a nickname.

### Embellish Your Own
Add color or texture to a simple pearl necklace by adding a few bows. Buy soft cotton fabric, lace, or ribbon from a craft store and tie a few bows at various points along the necklace.

# The Bouquet and the Boutonniere

The handcrafted bouquet and boutonniere are not made of flowers alone . . . they are made of memories, handpicked and pieced together. For example, an ordinary fabric bouquet wrap can be replaced with something more meaningful, like a piece of lace from your grandmother's or mother's wedding gown, or a fabric square from your favorite blanket when you were a kid.

If a loved one has passed away or is unable to attend due to other circumstances, pay tribute to him or her with a locket, strung with pretty ribbon. Place a photo of your loved one in the locket, wrap the ribbon around your bouquet, and carry it with you down the aisle on your wedding day. You can do the same with a favorite necklace from your fiancé or a vintage scarf from your mother.

Here are some more ideas for personalizing your bouquet.

### Monogrammed Handkerchief Wrap

A new handkerchief can be made personal with a blue monogram embroidered in the corner, or with an iron-on transfer monogram, found at most craft stores. Wrap it around your bouquet, and you have the comfort of knowing that, should the tears begin to flow, you have a handkerchief close at hand.

You can also dye an ordinary white handkerchief any color you like to fit in with your wedding palette using a fabric dye like Rit, found at any craft or grocery store. You can control the intensity of the hue by how long you leave the handkerchief in the dye. Wrap your brightly colored handkerchiefs around the bridal-party bouquets, securing them with pins.

### Pearl-Wrapped Bouquet

Pearls are a classic bridal look that will never go out of style. Channel your inner Audrey Hepburn with a string (or two) of pearls wrapped around your bouquet — it

will tie in perfectly with a 1920s black-and-white-themed wedding. Wrap the pearls around the bouquet, secure with clear thread and a small knot, and remember to remove them after the ceremony. After the wedding, you can wear the pearls on date nights, anniversaries, and other special occasions.

### Handpicked Bouquet

Is your favorite aunt known for her beautiful rose garden? Are your best friend's peonies out of this world? Instead of trying to figure out how she does it, enlist her help to provide a small, freshly picked bouquet right from her garden for you to carry down the aisle. Have the flowers cut right before the nuptials (or chilled the night before), tie them with a simple ribbon, and you're ready to go. Just as homemade food is so much better than store bought, so, too, are homegrown bouquets.

A boutonniere is a must-have for the groom, and it's easy to make. Consider crafting similar boutonnieres for the groomsmen, fathers, and grandfathers. I added a hair clip to the back (with a small dab of hot glue) in case the wearer wants to avoid pinning through fabric, they can just use the clip.

For this project, you'll need the following supplies for each boutonniere:

- **one large rose**
- **one sweetheart rose**
- **green stems**
- **reindeer moss** (available at craft stores)
- **craft glue** (I recommend Mod Podge)
- **jute twine**
- **scissors**
- **tan felt**
- **a pin back** (I recommend using one with an added round portion on top, which gives the boutonniere a stronger backing.)

1. Arrange the two roses, a leaf or two, and a bit of moss.

2. Tie with the jute twine at the top to secure the pieces. Do not cut the twine; leave one long length.

3. Wrap the twine from the top to the bottom.

4. Cut a small circle of the felt (the same size as the pin back) and glue to the back of the pin. After a couple of minutes, glue the pin back onto the back of the boutonniere. Press and hold for a minute or two. Use a dab of glue to attach the loose end of twine to the wrapping on back.

### Baby's-Breath Bouquet

Formerly known as a "filler flower," baby's breath has become quite the stunning bouquet choice. Gather plenty of it to make a bouquet, wrap floral tape around the stems to hold them tight, and cover the tape with burlap (for a rustic touch) or satin ribbon (for a pop of color).

### Carnation Bouquet

The carnation has made a comeback! Also thought of as a filler flower because they are so cheap, carnations are incredibly versatile. They are available in a rainbow of colors and are very sturdy, withstanding the cold of winter weddings as well as summer's heat and humidity. In big, tight bouquets, carnations can be stunning. Create carnation bouquets by gathering up bunches in your wedding colors — or

select a color for each bridesmaid in her favorite shade — and wrap the stems in floral tape. For a whimsical touch, wrap the stems with colorful fabric in coordinating prints and patterns.

## • FRESH-BOUQUET ALTERNATIVES •

Consider an unexpected fresh-bouquet alternative — forever bouquets, as I like to call them, because, quite honestly, they never die. A fresh-bouquet alternative is an excellent option for the bride who has allergies, can't justify spending hundreds of dollars on flowers only to see them wilt, or wants a keepsake memento of her flowers after the wedding day. Here are a few alternatives to fresh flowers that may be right for you.

### Silk Bouquets

Quality silk flowers look and almost feel like fresh flowers, and they last forever. However, to get the look that rivals the real thing, you'll need to spend a little more to obtain a higher-grade silk.

Another benefit of using silk flowers is that the flowers you want are always in season! So, brides, you no longer have to have a June wedding if you want to walk down the aisle carrying peonies.

Using silk flowers also allows you to customize your bridesmaid bouquets. If one of your bridesmaids loves tulips, another daisies, no problem; select a small bouquet of them and wrap the stems in ribbon or a handkerchief. The idea is to give each bridesmaid a custom bouquet "handpicked" just for her.

### Brooch Bouquet

This is a bouquet constructed of brooches strung on lengths of wire and attached together (sometimes paired with silk or fresh flowers). You can certainly make a brooch bouquet yourself out of jewelry from your own collection, as well as thrift-store and garage- and estate-sale finds. However, the brooch bouquet is an art form all its own; enlisting the help of a professional brooch-bouquet artisan (look for one online) is key in creating a one-of-a-kind bouquet. You can usually send your favorite brooches (if there are heirloom brooches you'd like to include), and the artisan will happily incorporate them into your piece.

### Button Bouquet

The button bouquet is created in a similar fashion to the brooch bouquet. Wire "stems" are shaped with pliers to look like branches, with the buttons mounted at various levels. For a fuller look, fabric floral blooms can be added. You can find button bouquets at www.Lillybuds.com.

### Pinwheel Bouquet

For a whimsical touch at an outdoor ceremony, have each bridesmaid carry a pinwheel down the aisle in lieu of a bouquet, and then place it in the ground at the end of the aisle. How fun!

### Origami-Paper Bouquet

For this bouquet, origami posies are attached to lengths of wire, which are stuck into a large Styrofoam ball. A wooden dowel inserted in the ball allows the bride to carry it down the aisle. Imagine all of those cleverly orchestrated paper shapes jam-packed into a punchy bouquet to enjoy forever!

### Flower Wand

Attach colorful satin ribbons to one side of a dowel with hot glue; on top of the ribbons, glue a large silk flower.

### In Lieu of a Bouquet

Who says you have to carry a bouquet?

The bottom line to the bouquet story is that whatever you want is fine. Don't limit yourself to certain materials or "traditional" styles. And if none of them suits your fancy, feel free to walk down the aisle holding nothing but your father's arm.

# The Groom

It's his day, too, and the groom should sport a style that suits him best . . . even if it isn't a suit. There are plenty of ways he can dress for his wedding day, incorporating handcrafted, meaningful details. While most of the attention will be on his bride, that doesn't mean he can't grab some of the style spotlight for himself!

## *A Secret Tag*

Sew a tag onto the back of your groom's tie or on the inside of his suit-jacket pocket before the wedding day. A secret message, such as "I Love You," "Can't Wait for the Aisle," his initials, or the wedding date will be a sweet surprise as he's getting ready before the ceremony. Secretly sneak the tie or suit coat away a few days before the wedding, have the tag sewn on, and put it back where you found it.

If you're sewing a special tag on the inside of his jacket pocket, tuck a love note inside the pocket for him to read on the morning of the wedding. He'll love it.

### Prevent Cold Feet

Keep him from getting cold feet with a custom pair of socks. Buy a pair of dress socks in his size (make sure they coordinate with his wedding attire); use an iron-on decal of (or hand embroider) his initials on the socks. Place the socks in a small box; tie a ribbon around it. Include a tag that reads, "From Your Bride"; this gift is certain to warm his heart and his feet.

Also, gift him a pair of wedding-day boxers. A comical pair (hearts, perhaps?) or an iron-on decal will make the gifting even more fun. Better yet, personalize them: a Web site like www.SpreadShirt.com lets you upload an original design or message.

### Wear a Bolo

If you're having a Western-themed wedding, a bolo would work better than a necktie. Have the groomsmen follow suit. Don't forget the cowboy boots!

### Cuff Links

A borrowed pair of cuff links from your fiancé's father, grandfather, favorite uncle, or friend will mean more to him than a store-bought pair.

Another special option is to make a custom pair of cuff links for your groom by buying cuff link "blanks" that have space for a tiny photo. Print a photo, the logo of a favorite sports team, or the insignia of his alma mater. He'll love wearing his custom cuff links — made by his beautiful bride — on the wedding day and beyond.

## Borrow a Vintage Suit

For starters, there's the idea of "something borrowed" for his attire. Was your husband's grandfather one hep cat? Was his great-uncle always dressed to the nines? Your fiancé can borrow a suit or buy one from a thrift or vintage store. Have it professionally cleaned and tailored for a flattering fit.

## Sentimental Tie

The groom can pay homage to his father, grandfather, or other notable person in his life by wearing a tie from their collection. It can be vintage or contemporary — whatever looks best with what your man will be wearing.

Or, if you purchased a tie for your groom during your courtship, suggest that he wear it on the wedding day.

## CHAPTER 3
# The Wedding Party

◄○►

If your wedding were a football game, the wedding party would be the starting lineup, ready to tackle anything that comes their way. This handpicked support system has been with you through it all, maybe even since the day you were born. The team is there to stand by your side and bolster you on this, the most important day of your life.

While bridesmaids and groomsmen may have a slightly different approach to the wedding preparations, the end goal is the same: a perfectly smooth day for the bride and groom.

With your wedding party being such a stellar group of individuals, make the wedding day worth their while by making them happy. Give them freedom when it comes to attire (within reason, of course), keep the itinerary to a minimum, and spoil them like crazy on the wedding day. You know they'd do the same for you.

# The Bridesmaids

The bridesmaids have two goals: to make sure the only tears the bride sheds are those of joy, and to guaranatee that everything goes smoothly (or, if it doesn't, that the bride never hears about it).

The maid/matron of honor is responsible for holding the bride's bouquet and straightening the bride's train whenever necessary throughout the ceremony. The bridesmaids should keep a supply of tissues handy for the bride, and one bridesmaid should hold the bride's purse or shawl, if needed.

Before the ceremony, the bridesmaids can distribute programs to guests as they arrive, and the groomsmen can escort guests to seats. Bridesmaids and groomsmen can also ensure that ceremony items are set up per your instructions, such as flowers or aisle décor.

In return, do all you can to make this a wonderful experience for your bridesmaids as well.

## • THE BRIDESMAID DRESS •

When selecting the bridesmaid dress, find one that you'd like to wear. If you wouldn't wear it, they shouldn't have to wear it, either. Here are some nontraditional options to consider.

### The Little Black Dress

One of my favorite bridesmaid-dress ideas is the little black dress. Most every bridesmaid will already have one in her closet, along with a pair of black shoes to match. Or, you can add a pop of color by asking bridesmaids to purchase heels in a particular shade.

### Mismatched Bridesmaid Dresses

While the idea of telling bridesmaids to wear any dress they like to your wedding sounds enticing, decide if you can truly handle a completely uncoordinated look —

for instance, one bridesmaid showing up in a floor-length ball gown, while another wears a cute short skirt. If that scenario makes you cringe, here are a few ways to pull off the eclectic look with elegance and sophistication, while still giving your girls a little leeway in fashion selection. Assign each bridesmaid a particular shade within a color palette. For instance, if soft pink is the color, those shades could be salmon, peach, blush, and nude. The result would be a coordinated range of hues within the same color family.

Or, you can select a specific shade and material, and then let your bridesmaids select their own dress styles. Some dress shops offer many styles of dress in a similar fabric and specific shade. That way, each bridesmaid can pick a style that works best for her, while still coordinating with everyone else in the bridal party.

### The Bridesmaid Skirt

For a spring or summer wedding, why not consider a more casual approach? Select a pretty patterned skirt for each bridesmaid to wear, and pair it with a solid tank top. You can dress up the look with heels, or dress it down with flip-flops or sandals.

### The Handmade Bridesmaid Dress

If you're interested in a handmade alternative with your unique personal style, make your own! Yes, that's right — I'm talking about made-from-scratch bridesmaid dresses. If you're not feeling quite that crafty — and few of us are — enlist the help of a seamstress. Find someone locally who is willing to work with your dress design. Together, you'll create a pattern you'll love, in the fabric best suited for the design. Have your bridesmaids measured, buy the fabric, and surprise them with a gift they can wear on the wedding day — and beyond.

If you don't have a design in mind, consult the Internet for seamstresses who offer vast collections of custom-made bridesmaid dresses. Thanks to the power of the Web, it's easier than ever to send measurements, color palettes, and preferences via e-mail. Plus, you have the flexibility of working one-on-one with the seamstress to discuss any questions over the phone, receive swatches by mail, and view photos from her collection, all without leaving the comfort of your own home. Once the dresses arrive, your bridesmaids can schedule an appointment with a tailor for a last-minute sizing to make sure the fit is perfect.

If you are having the dresses custom made, at the time you order them, you can provide the seamstress with heartfelt tags to be sewn into each dress, either in lieu of the standard dress tag or onto the hem. Buy a piece of fabric or embroidery cloth and hand stitch each woman's name or monogram, or a special message.

### Vintage Dress

If you're planning a vintage-themed wedding, consider bridesmaid dresses appropriate to a particular time period. Browse vintage dress shops and thrift stores with your girls to find fashionable frocks from the decade of your choosing.

## • GIFTS FOR THE BRIDESMAIDS •

Your bridesmaids spend time, money, and energy making sure your wedding day goes perfectly for you. Say thank you with a thoughtful gift they'll love.

### A Stylish Sash

Why not handcraft a sash for each of your bridesmaids' dresses? For a more formal look, craft them out of satin; and no matter what type of fabric you use, adorn them with whatever kind of embellishment you like — pearls, antique buttons, lace, sequins, rhinestones, feathers, or a vintage brooch. You can even give each one its own personal twist. For instance, if your best friend's favorite color is blue, add blue vintage buttons paired with lace.

### Clutch Purse

This is my favorite go-to bridesmaid gift, because I can't think of a single woman who doesn't love a new purse. Clutch purses are compact, versatile, and customizable in any color imaginable. You can also add a surprise message inside, like "Thanks for being my bridesmaid!" or "I found my guy, but I

still love my girls." In lieu of a sewn tag, you can place a handwritten note in each one, along with a few goodies like mints, her favorite lip gloss, and a disposable camera.

### Glassware

Mimosas on the wedding day are more fun when served up in hand-painted glassware. Use acrylic paint markers to customize wine or champagne glasses with your bridesmaids' names, a thematic element of the wedding, an inside joke, or a nickname.

### Charm Necklace

It's easy to create a silver or gold single-charm necklace. You'll need a sterling-silver box chain (approximately 18 inches long), a lobster clasp (and two jump rings), a pair of needle-nose pliers, and a charm or pendant that suits each bridesmaid, like an initial charm. Add the charm or pendant to the chain by threading the chain through the pendant ring; use the pliers and jump rings to attach the lobster clasp to the ends of the chain. Set it in colorful tissue paper in a jewelry box, and tie it up with a ribbon, along with a note expressing your thanks.

### Gemstone Satin Necklace

Craft a necklace by threading a satin ribbon through a gemstone bead, pearl bead, or other bauble of your choice.

### Lace Cuff Bracelet

A piece of satin fabric with a floral appliqué ironed onto it can become a bridesmaid cuff in a few easy steps. Iron the appliqué onto the satin fabric, glue a strip of lace on either side of the piece, and tie it in a bow around the wrist.

### Bead Earrings

You can make glam earrings using fanciful, decorative beads. Find beads with flat backs, and buy earring backs and closures. Use a hot-glue gun to add a dab of glue to the back of the bead; place an earring back on the glue and hold it in place at the opposite end with your fingers. (Be careful with the hot glue.) Allow it to cool for a few minutes, then place an earring closure on top. It's almost too easy to make these — you'll wonder why you've waited so long to start!

## • GETTING-READY GIFTS •

You already know what you'll be wearing on your wedding day, but what will you and your bridesmaids wear to get ready for it? Make sure what you wear won't undo hours of styling perfection, as a T-shirt removed over your head can snag your 'do or muss your mascara.

### Getting-Ready Shirts

Monogram the pockets of button-down shirts for your girls to add personalization, or add an iron-on appliqué with their initials or names to the backs of zippered hoodies.

### Sweet Sweaters

Cardigans — in coordinating colors — are easily embellished with fabric flower pins, sequins, vintage buttons, pearls, seed beads — anything that inspires you. Your bridesmaids will love to wear them while getting ready, plus they make for adorable snapshots and can be worn to keep cozy all night long. And since they don't have "bridesmaid" written all over them, they can be reworn after the wedding day.

### Spa Slippers

What goes together with a comfy, embellished cardigan? A pair of cozy spa slippers, of course! Give your girls the gift of happy, pain-free feet with a pair of handmade slippers. You can wear them while getting ready, then toss them into a tote bag to wear later on the dance floor. Most craft stores sell patterns to follow to make your own, or you can purchase a pair at a craft show or retail store. A pair of gray or black slippers will complement nearly any dress; don't forget a pair in white for you, too!

### Robe

A robe to wear while getting ready on the wedding day (and afterward) is one your bridesmaids will happily wear again. Look for robes made of a luxurious fabric like satin or silk, and have them monogrammed.

### Tote Bag

If there's one gift you plan on giving bridesmaids, let it be a tote bag. As a bridesmaid, there are five thousand tiny little things to carry around with you on the wedding day, and there is usually no great place to store it all. If you've ever been a bridesmaid, you know the feeling of running around, not quite knowing where you left your hairspray, gum, wallet, keys — you get the idea. Give your bridesmaids a custom, handmade tote bag to keep track of it all. Buy a solid canvas tote bag, fabric paint, stencils, and embellishments (flower pins, appliqués, iron-on monograms, rhinestones, etc.), and decorate each girl's bag. For a girly touch, you can sew pink ruffle ribbon onto the handle and cover the seams with decorative lace. Fill the tote bags with wedding-day essentials like tissues, travel-size hairspray, safety pins, bobby pins, clear nail polish to fix nylon runs, aspirin, gum, a pocket-size mirror, and a favorite lip gloss.

If you want to handcraft a piece of jewelry for each of your bridesmaids, earrings are a great and surprisingly easy choice.

For this project, you'll need the following supplies for each set of earrings:

- scissors
- ivory-colored felt
- hot-glue gun
- two plain 12mm buttons
- fabric (for a perfect match, if you're having the bridesmaids' dresses custom made, ask for a length of the fabric.)
- earring backs
- earring closures

Before you begin, cut two small circles of felt the same size as the buttons. Using hot glue, attach one piece of the felt to the back and one piece to the front of each button. Press firmly.

1. Cut two pieces of fabric big enough to cover the felt and button completely.

2. Use hot glue to attach the fabric to each of the buttons, turning slowly to ensure that the fabric is pulled tightly across the button. Hold the fabric in place until it's dry.

3. Glue one end of the earring back to each button; then attach the closure. Allow it to completely dry.

4. Pack the earrings in gift boxes, and present them to your bridesmaids on the wedding day.

# The Flower Girl

**T**he flower girl is one of the cutest members of your bridal party, rivaling only the ring bearer for the title.

In order to keep your flower girl happy throughout the wedding festivities, try to recall what it was like being her age. Do you remember being five years old and having to wear a fancy (and possibly not comfortable) dress for a holiday dinner? After a few hours, you were ready to put on your pajamas. Now, imagine being a flower girl in a wedding, where you have to wake up early after staying up too late the night before from excitement and nervousness, wear a fancy dress, and then try your absolute hardest not to spill anything on it. It's a tough job being a flower girl! Let's discuss a few ways you can make the occasion more meaningful for her, so it ends up being a day she'll remember fondly.

## • THE FLOWER-GIRL DRESS •

The key to selecting a dress for your flower girl? Comfort. Fluffy and frilly are fine, so long as the dress doesn't itch or irritate. If you want to use tulle, be sure there is a layer of soft fabric added underneath. If it's a more casual wedding, consider a sundress with a cotton sash, an eyelet dress with a lace bow, or a white tank top with a decorative rosette trim and a flowing tutu skirt. She'll feel like a princess. You can even detail a plain tank top yourself by adding lace appliqués, along with sequin trim. She'll love that it was handmade by the bride — too cool.

Don't forget to give the flower girl something to keep her warm. A plain white cardigan can be embellished with seed beads for added sparkle, or truly make it her own by having it embroidered with her monogram.

The flower girl's dress typically doesn't match those of the bridesmaids; most flower girls wear white, ivory, or pink. But if you'd like your flower girl to walk down the aisle sporting a miniature of the bridesmaid dress, go ahead — you're the bride, after all. Another option is have the flower-girl dress echo a feature of the bridesmaid dress — for instance, you could add a sash or floral pin, or have the flower girl wear a decorative headband in the same hue as the big-girl dresses.

## • FLOWER-GIRL GIFT IDEAS •

Give a gift your flower girl will love by finding out what she likes. Is she a girly girl who loves to play dress up and dreams of being a princess? Or is she a bookworm whose favorite place is the library? Or is she a tomboy who loves sports, chases after bugs, and isn't afraid to get muddy? Whatever it may be, find a perfect, personal gift for her that she'll love, and you'll totally make her day.

### Robe
Make her feel like one of the girls with a flower-girl robe to wear with the bridesmaids on the wedding day. Select a style suitable for her age, perhaps one with a favorite cartoon character or a pattern that represents something she likes to do (like ballet or soccer).

### Special Necklace
Craft a flower-girl necklace using white double-faced satin ribbon and large (19mm) pearl beads. Cut an 18-inch length of ribbon. Tie a knot 3 inches from one end; string a bead onto

the ribbon; tie a knot next to the bead as a spacer. Continue adding beads until approximately 3 inches from the other end; tie another knot. The necklace can now be tied with a bow to fit the flower girl.

### Decorated Hairpins

The flower girl will feel honored with a pair of hairpins crafted especially for her! To make them, you'll need two bobby pins, hot glue, cabochon rose beads, and two cabochon settings, one for each pin. Glue a cabochon setting to a bobby pin and press firmly until it's dry. Glue the cabochon bead to the setting until it's secure. Present the special hairpins in a wrapped gift box.

### Headband

Every flower girl can use a headband, particularly one that was custom made for her (see the DIY headband on page 39).

### Sparkly Shoes

What little girl wouldn't love a pair of sparkly shoes? Make her a pair by following the directions for glitter flats on page 34.

### Shoe Clips

You can dress up a pair of white flower-girl shoes with custom shoe clips, fashioned from small silk roses glued to alligator clips and fastened to the sides of her shoes.

### Wedding-Day Tote

Create a custom tote bag and fill it with a piece of jewelry to wear to the wedding, a selection of her favorite candy, a pack of crayons, and a coloring book. You'll be her hero. Or, for the book-loving girl, find out from her parents which series she's reading, and buy a book or two for her tote, complete with a book light. For the outdoorsy girl, fill up her tote bag with sidewalk chalk, a jump rope, and a bottle of bubbles.

# • THE ROLE OF THE FLOWER GIRL •

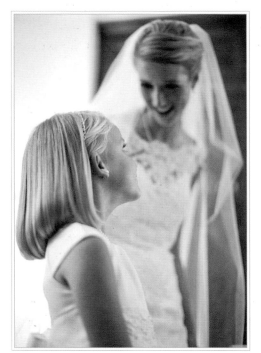

The flower girl's traditional role — besides looking adorable, naturally — is to toss flower petals down the aisle. I say, baskets with petals have held the spotlight for long enough; it's time to twist tradition a bit with alternatives the flower girl can carry.

## Jack-o'-Lantern

For a fall or Halloween-inspired wedding, have your flower girl carry a small pumpkin or carved jack-o'-lantern down the aisle. Use an LED candle for safety. Keep the pumpkin its natural color, or add a coat of metallic or glitter spray paint. Autumn leaves made of paper can become the new "rose petals."

## Farm-Inspired Basket

I live in a small town where peaches are a big deal. And, when I say a big deal, I mean there's an entire week dedicated to a festival of peaches. If you're planning a homespun woodland- or farmland-inspired wedding, feature homegrown foods by using bushels of fresh fruit throughout your décor. For the flower girl, fill a small basket with a few peaches, corn husks, or apples in lieu of flowers, with the emphasis placed on items that are light enough for her to carry comfortably down the aisle.

## Lantern

Have your flower girl carry a lightweight lantern, with a battery-operated light instead of a candle. Add colorful fillers like hot-pink sand, a few gemstones, or seashells. Let her lead the way down the aisle with light rather than petals.

### Wand

A flower-girl wand will make her feel like a princess. Create a wand by wrapping ribbon in any shade you like around a wooden dowel, hot gluing it as you wrap. Once you reach the end, glue a few ribbons to the top, making sure the strips are long enough for your flower girl to twirl.

### A Love Note

Before the ceremony, write a short love note for your groom; fold it in half and have the flower girl carry it down the aisle to the groom.

### Sentimental Symbols

Have your flower girl help you share your love story. For instance, if you met your husband in high school, she can carry your school yearbook down the aisle.

If your groom is a talented guitarist, he may wish to play a song as part of your wedding ceremony. Your flower girl could carry the guitar pick or sheet music down the aisle.

### The Vows

Instead of tucking your vows in a pocket, place them in a box and have your flower girl carry it down the aisle. The box can become a keepsake to house your vows after the wedding.

### Announce the Bride's Arrival

Have your flower girl walk down the aisle, holding a banner or sign that says, "Here Comes the Bride." This idea is charming, sentimental, and functional, all rolled into one.

### The Train

Your flower girl can help the maid of honor carry your train down the aisle. Walk very slowly so she can keep up. Once you get to the end of the aisle, have her place the train gently on the ground (and provide plenty of practice at rehearsal so she's confident). (This idea reminds me of planning my own wedding. When I was trying on wedding dresses, I stood on a dress pedestal — the kind with mirrors all around — to show my mom how the train looked. Without any hesitation, a flower girl from another bridal party walked over to admire the gown, reached down, and fluffed the dress out. She looked up and smiled at me ever so sweetly!)

# The Groomsmen

Just as the bride has her girls, the groom has his guys. The groom hand selects his groomsmen, a group of friends he's known since birth (such as a brother or cousin), kindergarten, or college, with perhaps a new buddy from work. Unlike bridesmaids, groomsmen don't spend the morning of the wedding at the salon getting ready… which means this is a perfect opportunity for the gentlemen to take part in a little male bonding. The handcrafted wedding isn't about details alone; it's about the moments and memories you create along the way. The groom should use this time to do something fun with the groomsmen before suiting up for the ceremony.

If your groom is an avid golfer, he and his groomsmen can hit the links for a few rounds. If he wants to channel his inner twelve-year-old, he could arrange for a game of laser tag or paintball early in the morning. Planning a beachfront wedding? Arrange for a fishing trip. Maybe the groomsmen will even be up for a little croquet tournament before the guests arrive.

The best man is most notably responsible for standing alongside the groom throughout the ceremony and having possession of the rings until the couple is ready to exchange

vows. The best man should make sure the groom gets to the ceremony on time, fully dressed, and should prevent him from seeing the bride before the wedding (unless the couple prefers otherwise).

The groomsmen are responsible for making sure the groom has the correct clothing items before the ceremony (the right size shirt and pants, a tie, and proper dress socks) and keeping him cool and calm. I heard of a wedding where the groom's outfit was delivered just hours before the ceremony, and the pants and shirt didn't fit. The groomsmen worked together to find the proper sizes in record time.

### • GROOMSMEN ATTIRE •

Just as the morning-of rituals vary from wedding to wedding, so does the attire of the groomsmen. Since your wedding isn't the same as everyone else's, consider attire to suit your style. After the groom decides what he'll wear, plan a cohesive wardrobe for the groomsmen.

### The Tie

Instead of a formal tuxedo or suit, the groomsmen can wear a dress shirt, a tie, and a vest. A traditional tie is fine, but a custom tie is more personal. Hand-printed neckties with custom initials, whiskey labels, bicycles, beehives, antlers, tire tracks, or sailing ships all sound like way more exciting options than your standard tie (you can find them at www.Cyberoptix.com).

### When the Weather Is Warm

For a formal look in warmer weather, groomsmen could wear a vest and button-down shirt instead of a sport coat; or, skip the vest for suspenders paired with a necktie.

A beach or other casual wedding might call for a white linen short-sleeve shirt, khaki shorts, and sandals.

## *Cowboy Couture*

For a Western-themed wedding, the groomsmen can wear a button-down shirt with a bow tie, necktie, or no tie, paired with denim jeans and cowboy boots.

## • GIFTS FOR THE GROOMSMEN•

When considering gifts for the groomsmen, think about items that are useful and customizable. I prefer wearable items that can be worn on the wedding day. Here are some of my favorite ideas.

## *Cuff Links*

These are fun because you can customize them to suit each groomsman's taste and interests. If the groom and his buddies constantly quote a particular movie, can't get enough of a certain band, or want to wear their college days on their sleeve with

their college insignia, custom cuff links let you do that. Cuff-link "blanks" can be purchased online or at craft stores. Look for the ones with a clear frame in front, which can hold a photograph cut down to size. Just print, glue, and assemble the cuff links, then wrap and present them to the groomsmen on the wedding day.

### *Wallet*

A handmade leather wallet makes a great gift for groomsmen. A wallet is one of those items that will get used until it literally begins to fall apart.

## *Bow Tie*

If your groomsmen prefer bow ties to neckties, consider gifting them a set of custom bow ties that matches the color of the bridesmaids' dresses, or hand select a bow tie for each groomsman to fit his style and personality.

## *Pocket Squares*

A pocket square is a classic accessory that never goes out of style. If you're a needle-crafter, you can embroider each groomsman's initials onto a white pocket square.

### Shaving Kit

A shaving kit, complete with shaving soap and a razor, makes a great gift for the groomsmen.

### Pocket Watch

A pocket watch is as stylish as it is functional. Engrave the back or the inside of the front cover for a personal touch, and wrap it in a small wooden box secured with twine.

### Bottle Opener

A bottle opener engraved with the groomsman's initials makes for a very functional gift. Add a key chain to it, and you'll be assured that he'll carry it with him at all times.

### Belt Buckle

A custom belt buckle with his monogram can be worn on the wedding day and afterward.

### Unique Thematic Gifts

If the groomsmen enjoy football together, gift them with jerseys of their favorite players. Are they college buddies? Think about college gear — a college tee, engraved flask, coffee mug, or tickets to an upcoming football game. Do they like to go fishing? A set of lures or hand-tied dry flies is a nice way to say thanks for being a groomsman.

Other favorite gift ideas include cigars with a cigar cutter and engraved lighter, a unique coffee-table book, a collectible item (i.e., a vintage record not yet part of his collection), a fine bottle of liquor, or even a new pair of kicks if the groomsmen will be wearing them on the wedding day in lieu of traditional dress shoes.

# The Ring Bearer

The ring bearer is the little guy of the groomsman group. He's dressed just like the "big guys," knows his role is pretty important, and he, too, thinks the groom is one of the coolest guys ever. Make sure he feels as special as he is with custom, handmade details.

Make your ring bearer feel like one of the guys by selecting a pair of pants, jacket, shirt, and tie to match the groomsmen. If your little man isn't a fan of a bow tie or necktie, opt instead for no tie and just a suit coat. After all, you don't want your ring bearer coming down the aisle in tears.

Or, instead of a suit or tuxedo, he can wear a polo shirt and a pair of dress pants. If it's a more informal wedding, let him wear cargo shorts and a linen button-down shirt, so he's comfortable enough to perform his special task with confidence.

## • RING-BEARER GIFT IDEAS •

You want to give the ring bearer a gift that's suitable for his age and makes him feel like a special part of the wedding party.

### Teddy Bear

Build your ring bearer his own personal bear. Purchase a small teddy bear and "dress" him with doll accessories (available at a craft store) in a custom outfit. Use fabric paint (with a fine-point tip) or an acrylic marker to write "Ring Bearer Bear" on the front of the bear's shirt. He'll love it.

### Tote Bag

Fill a tote bag with his favorite things: consider a coloring book, crayons, a yo-yo, and a kid's camera.

### Ring-Bearer Superhero

The ring bearer plays an important role in your ceremony. Make him feel like he saved the day with his favorite superhero cape — or, better yet, make him a custom ring bearer cape! Buy fabric (approximately 20 inches long) and fashion it into a cape. Use Velcro so he can attach the sides easily and comfortably. Add an iron-on appliqué with a ring and his initials, name, or "Ring Bearer." Don't be surprised if he wants to wear it down the aisle!

## • THE ROLE OF THE RING BEARER•

The role of the ring bearer is to carry the rings down the aisle on a pillow and hand them to the best man. You can certainly buy a pillow for this use, but it's also an opportunity for some hand-crafted details.

### "Something Old"

Craft your own ring pillow using satin fabric and pillow fill. Once it's complete, sew a vintage handkerchief (your great-grandmother's, perhaps) onto the top of the pillow. Tie a ribbon through the center and attach the rings to it.

### *"Something New"*

Craft your pillow using fabric from your gown if there are any leftovers. Even if you don't save your gown, you'll always have a piece of its fabric to cherish on the pillow. For decoration, sew vintage buttons or pearls to the top.

### *"Something Borrowed"*

For "something borrowed" utilize an heirloom ring pillow from your grandmother, mother, or a friend.

### *"Something Blue"*

Craft a pillow with a single length of blue ribbon running across the top. Or buy a vintage handkerchief with a blue pattern and sew it onto your ring pillow.

### *Rustic Ring Pillow*

Wrap a small pillow in burlap and sew the edges together securely. Tie jute or twine in a bow around the middle and attach the rings to it. For embellishment, pin a hand-made fabric flower or vintage brooch to the top.

## • RING-PILLOW ALTERNATIVES •

Instead of a ring pillow, have the ring bearer carry something nontraditional. Here are some fun, unexpected ring-pillow alternatives to try.

### *Box*

A wooden cigar box — sanded, painted, and repurposed — is a great choice for carrying rings down the aisle. Unlike a ring pillow, with only a ribbon to secure the rings, the box keeps them snug inside, minimizing the possibility of any ring mishaps. Plus, it's easy for the best man to simply open the box and remove the rings.

### *Books*

A small stack of hardcover books — perhaps shared favorite reads or books of poetry — can be tied up in ribbon with a bow at the top. Tie the rings to the ribbon and have him carry the stack down the aisle, to be placed on a small table nearby.

Or combine the idea of the ring-bearer box and book with a hollow book safe (available at www.conduit-press.com). You can place the rings inside the book to be carried down the aisle; after the wedding, use the box to stash your love notes to one another.

### Sand Dollar

If you're planning a beach-themed wedding, a sand dollar can be used in lieu of a ring pillow. Tie a ribbon around the sand dollar, then string the ribbon ends through your rings and tie a loose knot.

### Antique Jewelry Box

Consider using a small, antique jewelry box as your ring-bearer pillow by simply placing the rings inside.

### Nest

Create a nature-inspired ring pillow with a decorative bird nest and reindeer moss (both available at a craft store). A ribbon is tied tightly around the nest into a knot, with the rings secured to the top in a bow. This lightweight ring pillow is perfect for small hands to carry.

This ring pillow measures about 8 inches wide and has a folded design that makes it look like an envelope.

For this project, you'll need the following supplies:

- a piece of linen fabric (about 11 inches wide x 17 inches long)
- a piece of blue silk dupioni, the same size as above
- thread to match the linen and the silk dupioni, plus a needle
- hot-glue gun
- wide stretchy lace ribbon, about 6 inches (I used a headband from Julie Comstock — see p. 39 for Web site address — because of its stretch, it worked well)
- polyfill stuffing
- thin satin ribbon to either match the blue silk dupioni or the stretchy lace ribbon, about 12 inches

Before you begin, machine stitch all edges of the linen and silk dupioni under about one-half inch. Lightly press with an iron.

1. Place the piece of linen out in front of you lengthwise. Fold up about 6 inches (a little less than one-third of the way up), making an "envelope" shape. Stuff with the polyfill until it's the thickness you desire.

2. Fold over the top of the linen envelope.

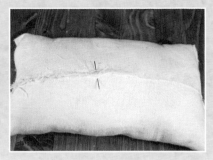

3. Hand stitch the two sides of the envelope, and then across the top to hold in the fill.

4. Place the linen pillow on the wrong (inside) side of the silk dupioni and fold in the edges as shown in the photograph above.

5. Continue folding and secure each new folded corner with a dab of hot glue.

6. Fold over the top of the silk dupioni envelope and secure with a dab of hot glue.

7. Wrap the wide stretchy lace ribbon tightly around the pillow and secure the ends on the back of the pillow with a dab of hot glue.

8. Turn the pillow over to the front and thread the thin satin ribbon through the lace.

9. String your rings onto the ribbon and tie (but not too tight) a bow. You want to safely secure the rings but make sure you can easily undo the ribbon when the time comes.

Create your own ring plate with moss set atop a decorative clay plate. After the wedding day, you can use the plate in your garden as a memento.

## For this project, you'll need the following supplies:

- craft glue, such as Mod Podge
- a terra-cotta dish, 6 inches in diameter
- small-size sponge brush
- reindeer moss (available at Jo-Ann stores)
- raffia
- scissors

1. Spread glue on the inside of the dish with the sponge brush.

2. Place handfuls of moss inside the dish and gently press down to secure them.

3. Once the area is entirely covered, take two strips of raffia and tie them both together in a knot across the plate, as you would a present.

4. Taking two of the raffia ends together, string the rings onto them, then tie them into an easy-to-undo bow with the other two raffia ends.

# CHAPTER 4

# The Ceremony

—◦—

Where do you dream of tying the knot? You can get married on the beach, in the woods, on a farm, in a church or synagogue, or in your own backyard. Any perfect ceremony location can benefit from the inclusion of handcrafted details. In this chapter, I'll identify ways to personalize your space and reflect your story in any setting.

# The Aisle

Whether you're holding an indoor or an outdoor wedding, the aisle usually sets the tone for the entire day's celebrations.

I tied the knot in Michigan in December, our ideal time for a holiday theme. We decorated the ceremony site with mistletoe, tied with red velvet ribbons. The aisle decorations included swags of evergreen studded with pinecones and holly. I saved the decorations and still use them in my home; there's nothing quite like finding décor you'll be able (and eager) to reuse after the wedding. Keep that in mind when selecting your pieces.

Here are some more ideas for decorating the aisle.

## Aisle Runner

Create your own aisle runner. Measure the length of your aisle and find a fabric to suit the space and surrounding decorations. Use stencils and paint (applied with a sponge brush) to add custom detailing, such as your initials, the wedding date, or your wedding logo.

An aisle runner can also be as simple as unadorned white fabric: no fuss, no muss.

### *Flower Cones*

A flower cone — also known as a petal cone — is a paper or fabric cone used as a container for flower petals. Or, you can transform it into a hanging cone by attaching a ribbon handle. Fill it with flower petals or potpourri, and it can be hung from the back of each ceremony chair. Or have your flower girl carry it down the aisle.

### *Candlelight Lanterns*

If you're having an evening wedding, you have the opportunity to revel in the romantic glow of candlelight (or LED candlelight, if safety is a concern). Place candles in glass containers (i.e., hurricane lanterns, jars, or decorative lanterns) and set them along the aisle.

### *Flower-Filled Jars*

Imagine your favorite flowers lining the way as you walk down the aisle to meet your future spouse — jars of peonies, lilies, daisies, sunflowers. To craft them yourself, fill each jar one third full with water, place the flowers inside, wrap wire around the top of the jar to create a handle, and tie on a ribbon for a pretty bow. If your wedding is outside and the ground is soft enough to do so, insert small shepherd's hooks along the aisle and hang your jars from their wire handles. After the ceremony, transport the flower-filled jars to the reception site as décor for the head table.

Instead of shepherd's hooks lining the aisle, an eco-friendly alternative is to gather manageable fallen branches, with a sturdy central limb that can be inserted into the ground. On one of the thicker branches, hang a small, lightweight jar filled with bunches of wildflowers or baby's breath. Repeat this same design to create a row of beautiful hanging bouquets.

### Wreaths

Place small wreaths along the aisleway. Decorative twig wreaths from a craft store can be embellished with seasonal touches such as moss or ivy in the spring, or metallic ornaments and sprigs of holly berries in the winter.

## • UNIQUE CEREMONY SEATING •

Do you have to follow conventional seating arrangements? Not always. Consider an alternative that suits your taste and your venue, using a few of these offbeat ideas.

### Pick a Seat, Not a Side

Instead of the soon-to-be-spouses' families picking sides, place a sign outside the ceremony site that tells guests to pick a seat — not a side — as both families are joining as one.

### Bales of Fun

An outdoor wedding with a more rustic feel might opt for ceremonial seating on hay bales instead of folding chairs. While it's a fun idea, keep two things in mind: first, cover the bales with fabric or blankets, so your guests don't end up with straw all over them; and second, choose this option for a short ceremony, as hay bales don't make for the most comfortable seating.

### Every Seat Is Front Row

For an intimate wedding ceremony, seat guests in a circle, so everyone has a front-row view of the nuptials.

### Reserved Seating

While planning the ceremony seating, don't forget to include "reserved" signs or notices, if needed. You can simply hang a "reserved" sign at the end of the rows where special seats have been saved. Or for a more subtle approach, use pink ribbons on the reserved seats instead of white, for example, to signify a reserved section.

## Programs and Other Ceremony Accoutrements

A ceremony program typically shares the names of the bridal party, describes the various parts of the ceremony, and can include song titles of music to be played during the ceremony. But there is no reason for yours to be typical. For instance, I once received a program with caricatures of the bridal party drawn by the groom. It described who each bridal party attendant was and why he or she was a special part of the couple's lives. The groom was able to share his love for art with the guests through the ceremony program, an item that is sometimes overlooked in wedding preparations.

### Print-Your-Own Program

An easy DIY ceremony program can be printed from your computer onto colorful card stock, cut into a particular shape (like a heart or circle, for instance), and glued to a wood craft stick to create a fan. This can be a practical option for summertime weddings, as a way for guests to keep themselves cool.

Include a personalized touch in your program by telling guests why you selected this particular venue, or why a ceremony song has significance to you. Or share your love story with a short piece on how you met.

What if a program isn't your style? You can still get guests involved in the ceremony in other ways.

### Sunglasses

Offer cheap sunglasses in baskets for guests to take, if your wedding is outdoors and the day is particularly sunny. Include a sign that reads something like "Our Future's So Bright, You'll Need These." Make sure you have handpicked pairs for you and the groom, and provide plenty of disposable cameras to capture everyone on film.

### Flags

Create whimsical flags — using textile remnants cut into squares and glued to dowels — for guests to wave as the couple proceeds down the aisle.

### Bubbles

Instead of tossing rice, blow bubbles! Buy bubble favors (with wands included) at a craft store. Place a bubble bottle at each seat, with a tag instructing guests to blow bubbles at the couple at the end of the ceremony.

### Birdseed

For an outdoor wedding, have the guests toss birdseed in celebration of the couple. Create small packets using white glassine bags; stamp the front with your wedding monogram. Fill each packet with birdseed and seal it with a sticker or wax seal. Place the packets on the guests' chairs before the ceremony begins or in a decorative basket at the door for guests to take as they enter the ceremony site.

### Confetti

Preloaded confetti shooters in plastic champagne bottles are fun to unleash on the couple as they make their way down the aisle. These bottles can be found at www. Save-on-Crafts.com (provided your venue doesn't mind the mess).

### Petals

Why should the flower girl have all the fun? Place small packets of fake petals — found at Michael's or Jo-Ann stores — and instructions for guests to toss them at the couple.

## Distribute these delightful

handkerchief favors to guests at your ceremony who may be sheeding a few "tears of joy." You could also place these favors in a basket, set outside the door of the ceremony, so guests can help themselves to them.

### For this project, you'll need the following supplies:

- **handkerchiefs** (buy them in packs)
- **kraft tags with a punched hole** (available at Jo-Ann stores)
- **black marker pen** (I use a black calligraphy pen by Martha Stewart from Michael's)
- **ribbon** (a 12-inch length per favor)

To begin, fold each handkerchief into a square, first folding it lengthwise in half, then folding it down.

1. On a kraft tag, write "For Tears of Joy" with the pen.

2. Loop a length of ribbon through the hole in the tag; then wrap it around the handkerchief.

3. Tie the ribbon in a knot at the back of the handkerchief.

# The Vows

Whether you write your own or recite traditional wedding vows, you can add a personal touch to the delivery of the vows, both at the ceremony and afterward, in your love nest.

*Notebook*

While planning your wedding, purchase two small (4 x 5-inch) notebooks. Cover them by cutting decorative paper (like scrapbook or kraft paper) to encompass the front cover, spine, and back cover of each book. Use hot glue to secure it in place; trim any excess around the edges. On the front, use a black permanent marker to write your initials, monogram, "Our Vows," or your wedding date. Glue a ribbon (6 inches in length, so it's visible on the outside of the book) to the inside of the back cover and use it as a bookmark. Write your vows inside the book to recite at your wedding; gift the other notebook to your groom so he can follow suit.

## Box

Instead of your pocket, place your vows in a customized wooden box. Use a wood-burning tool to engrave your names on the front, and line the inside with a pretty fabric, lace, or paper. Ask a close friend or family member to carry the box down the aisle during the procession or to present the box when it is time to recite your vows. After the wedding, put your written vows back in the box and keep them in a special place in your home. That way you'll always remember the vows you made.

## Turn Your Vows into a Keepsake

After the wedding, create a keepsake from your vows. Type your vows, then print them from your computer onto linen paper and frame them.

Select one line from your vows and have it engraved on a silver bracelet.

Make a custom canvas — created by you or ordered online — to hang on the wall so you can display your vows.

## • HONORED GUESTS •

Ask special friends or family members to be a part of the ceremony by reciting a poem, singing a song, or offering a particular talent.

### Music
If a family member or friend is a vocalist or musician, ask if he or she would play the music for your grand entrance or sing a particular song as part of the ceremony.

### Poem
Ask a special person to recite a poem for the ceremony.

### In Loving Memory
Whenever possible, make your ceremony more memorable by paying tribute to people who are important to you.

To honor a special person who cannot attend, ask a friend to carry a framed photograph of him or her down the aisle and place it on a table during the ceremony.

As a sign of remembrance, place a framed photograph or a bouquet of flowers at a reserved ceremony seat.

### Mothers/Fathers/Grandparents
Honor these family members during the ceremony with a small token of your appreciation. Consider a single flower or a handkerchief handed to them by the bride or groom.

## • SYMBOLS OF UNITY •

If you'd like to symbolize unity during your ceremony, there are various ways to personalize this tradition.

### Candle
A bride and groom can each hold a candle; then, together they can join the flames from their candles to light one new, central candle. The new candle is a symbol of their two lives united as one.

### Water
The couple pours a small amount of water from two glasses into one central cup; each individual takes a sip to symbolize their unity.

### Sand

Another way to represent the symbolic joining of two lives is with a sand ceremony, in which the bride and groom each pour a container of sand into a single, larger container.

### Salt Covenant

A salt covenant involves two small bags of salt and a glazed egg. The couple places their salt packets into the opening of the ceramic egg, combining them as one to symbolize their unity. You can find a raku egg and salt packets for this ceremony at www.CenteredCeramics.net.

### Potted Tree/Flower Plant

Each individual pours a small amount of water into a small potted tree or plant to show their unity. The tree or flower is then placed in the couple's home after the wedding, to symbolize strong roots as the foundation of a fruitful marriage.

### Bell

I read about a couple who rang a small bell during the unity portion of the ceremony, to symbolize the moment their bond was sealed through marriage. After the wedding, the bell was placed in the couple's home as a reminder of their bond.

### Love Letters

Write a letter to each other before the wedding, and place them in a box during the unity ceremony. On your first anniversary, open the box, read the letters, and save them as a keepsake.

# CHAPTER 5
## The Reception

—◁○▷—

At this point, you probably have an idea of how you'd like your special day to look. You've considered a theme, thought about the engagement announcements, the invitations, your gown, who you'd like for attendants, planned a preliminary guest list, etc. And now, you want to think about planning the biggest party of your life: The Reception.

Like the ceremony and everything else that has preceded this chapter, your reception should tie in memories and heartfelt, personal details for guests to notice — and remember. Here are some fun, creative ways to make your reception unforgettable.

# Décor

Customizing your wedding décor is one of the easiest ways to turn an ordinary wedding into a handcrafted one. If you put your whole heart into the details, guests are certain to notice.

## Monogram

Your monogram is your own personalized wedding fingerprint; use it to add custom touches to your favors, centerpieces, programs, invitations, and anywhere else you see fit.

You can create a "metallic" monogram using papier-mâché letters and silver or gold spray paint. Apply a coat of spray paint to the letters, covering them evenly on all sides. Apply a second coat; allow them to dry for 24 hours. You can stand the letters upright on any table — your cake table, guest-book table, or head table. Or display them on a wall, securing them with double-sided tape. And you don't have to limit yourself to your monogram — "Joy," "Love," "Just Married," and "XOXO" are other options.

## Decorative Chair Backs

Adorn the backs of the reception chairs with fabric or ribbon to add a whimsical touch. Buy a few spools of coordinating colors to tie into your décor, cut them into lengths, and gently knot the ends to each chair back, so you have multiple ribbons hanging from each chair down to the floor. I love how this looks, but it is time consuming to do it to every guest's chair. Plus, removing the ribbons at the end of the night will take a considerable amount of time. Instead, save time (and sanity) by reserving this idea for the backs of just the bride's and groom's chairs, or those of the bridal party.

You can also create ribbon or fabric floral garlands for your and your hubby-to-be's chair backs.

## Photographs

Give guests a glimpse into your courtship with a photograph board. Mount photographs onto a whiteboard (use rubber cement, as it dries clear). Place the whiteboard on an easel at the entryway of your reception for guests to view upon arrival. Or, instead of using a whiteboard, mount the photos on a banner that you string across a table.

You can also display your family lineage with a family tree or photographs of your parents and grandparents from their weddings. Have the photographs framed and placed on a table, along with a photograph of you and your new spouse as the latest married couple in the bunch.

### Wedding Banner

Chipboard letters or numbers, precut and sturdy, make fashioning a decorative banner a piece of cake. Available at craft stores, they can be covered with fabric or spray painted. Then, using ribbon and glue, attach them to one another to spell out anything you'd like, such as "Enjoy" above a dessert buffet; "Just Married" for your cake table; "Best Wishes" above your guest-book stand; "The Entourage" above the bridal-party table; your initials joined with an ampersand; or the wedding date.

### Chic Chair Banners

In the same way, using chipboard letters, create banners that will be used as chair markers. Spell out the name of each bridal party member on his or her chair back. For your own chairs, you can either spell out your names, "Mr." and "Mrs.," or "Bride" and "Groom." At one wedding I attended, a large ampersand was tied between the bride's and groom's chairs with satin ribbon. It looked cute and required no additional words.

You can also create personalized chair banners for the mothers and fathers of both the bride and groom, to make their seats extra special.

### Decorative Backdrops

You can use crepe paper in a similar fashion as wall décor behind the head table or dessert table. Crepe paper is lightweight and easy to anchor to nearly any surface. You can also hang crepe-paper strands from tree branches for a pop of color at an outdoor venue.

### Hanging-Lantern Jars

Wrap jelly jars in burlap and suspend them from branches outdoors using twine. Not only will the lanterns add a rustic flair to your wedding, but the light will help guide guests along pathways, to the restrooms, and to the parking lot with ease.

Wrapping papier mâché
letters with colorful yarn gives them a bolder effect.
To display on a wall at your wedding reception,
attach a lace or ribbon loop on the back.

For this project, you'll need the following supplies:

- yarn in two colors, one for each letter
- two papier mâché letters, one for each initial
- hot-glue gun

1. Tie the yarn in a knot at any end
   of the letter to secure it. Be sure
   to pull tightly so it doesn't come
   undone.

2. Wrap the letter with yarn, keeping
   the yarn tight and close up
   against the previous wrap.

3. Keep wrapping until the entire letter
   is covered. Cut the yarn and secure
   it to the letter with hot glue.

   Depending on the shape of the
   letter, you may need to cut the
   yarn at certain points, then tie the
   yarn on and begin again on
   another section of the letter. If you
   do, secure your cut end to the
   papier mâché surface with hot glue.

# The Guest Book

The guest book isn't just sheets of paper with signatures. It is a keepsake — a time capsule to be cherished and revisted, filled with sweet, heartfelt messages from those closest to you.

First, though, you need to properly set up your guest-book table. Position the table in a central location so guests see it as they enter the reception, and be sure to provide enough supplies (pens, film, stamps, etc.) for whatever type of "guest book" you've planned to use. If you choose to go with a nontraditional guest book, include easy-to-follow instructions, so your guests understand what you'd like them to do. Most important, ensure that there is ample lighting, so guests can see what they are writing.

Here are some of my favorite guest book ideas:

### Mad Libs

Create a custom Mad Libs sheet as a guest-book alternative. Write a short story about your wedding day, with plenty of blank spaces and prompts for guests to fill in nouns, adjectives, and words of wisdom. Print off a stack of them, and ask every guest to fill one in and sign it.

### Typewriter

If you're planning a wedding theme from a bygone era, consider having guests type their messages on a vintage typewriter, instead of using a pen and paper. Place a sheet of paper in the typewriter (with a basket nearby containing extra sheets), include a sign with instructions, and let guests type away.

### Coffee Mugs

A cute idea for the couple that loves their caffeine is to display a set of mugs labeled "Mr." and "Mrs.," with permanent markers for guests to sign their names onto the surface of each. Every day, the two of you can enjoy a hot cup of coffee, personalized by your loved ones. What a nice way to start off the morning!

### Remember When . . .

A memorable guest book is one that invites your guests to share memories. Custom card stock note cards printed with the words "Remember When . . . " across the top will give guests an opportunity to tell a story about the bride, the groom, or the couple together.

Decorate a box — a cigar box, for example — for guests to deposit their completed memory cards. After the wedding, have the cards placed into a scrapbook, to collect the beautiful — and funny — words shared by guests.

### Monogram Guest Book

Create a wooden monogram guests can sign; display it in your home after the big day. Buy large wooden letters (or create your own with plywood and a jigsaw), and sand and paint them. Have guests sign them, using permanent markers in a color that shows up well against whatever shade you've painted the letters.

### Poster

Draw, print, or custom order a poster — 11 x 14 inches or larger — with your new last name across it in open block letters. Have guests sign their names inside the block letters. Display it in your home after the wedding.

### Photo-Booth Guest Book

One of my favorite guest books is also a wedding favor — the photo-booth guest book. If you're planning to have a photo booth at your wedding, have two photos printed out: one for guests to take home as a favor, and one to be placed in your guest book. On your guest-book table, include scrapbook photo-adhesive stickers, pens, and a blank photo album with space for a short message or caption. Instruct guests to place their photos in the album using the stickers, sign their names, and include a caption. After the event, you'll have a beautiful wedding-day scrapbook containing hilarious visuals from throughout the festivities, group photos, and candid moments captured by guests, along with heartfelt messages.

Another photo idea is to enlarge a favorite photo of you and your sweetheart to an 8 x 10- or 11 x 14-inch size, and have it matted (using a light-colored mat) and framed, but without the glass. Place it on an easel, along with fine-point markers, for guests to sign their names on the matted portion.

### Quilted with Love

Buy plenty of quilt squares from a craft or fabric store, and place a stack of them on a table. Have each guest write his or her name on a square with a fabric marker. After the wedding, sew the squares together to make an memory quilt.

### Gardening Stones

Gather stones, clean them up, and place them at your guest-book table. In lieu of a book, guests will each write his or her name on a stone with permanent marker. Have guests put the signed stones in a galvanized tub or bucket for you to transport home. Place the stones throughout your garden for a lovely memory of the day.

### Song List

The gift of music is a beautiful one. Purchase a journal for guests to sign their names and list their favorite song and the artist. After the wedding, download the tracks and listen to them on your honeymoon. You'll laugh, you'll cry, and you'll be fascinated by the songs your guests have deemed favorites. Plus, you'll have a perfect wedding soundtrack to always remember, hand selected by your guests.

## A Favorite Book

Have guests sign a guest book of another kind: your favorite read. A favorite book of poetry, a classic novel, a book of quotes, or a collection of proverbs can become a keepsake signed by guests from your wedding. Place the book on a table with pens, and ask guests to flip through and sign their names anywhere they wish.

## Words of Advice

I have been at weddings where the DJ begins to play a song and invites all the married couples to the dance floor to share in a dance with the bride and groom. As the song progresses, couples married less than two years are asked to exit the dance floor, followed by couples married five years, ten years, fifteen, twenty . . . and so on. Eventually, the only couples left are the bride and groom and the longest-married couple in the room. When the song ends, the DJ asks the longest-married couple to share their advice for a happy marriage with the bride and groom.

Now, imagine that instead of signatures in your guest book, you ask guests for words of advice. Some guests may draw on personal experiences; others will give a hilarious response that will make you smile. But each answer will be from the heart, written for you both on your wedding day.

To give guests a chance to share their advice, create a guest-book journal. Buy a blank journal and write a question at the top of each page for guests to flip through and answer. They might include: "What is the key to a happy marriage?" or "What is your favorite-date night suggestion?" Questions or topics should be simple, heartfelt, and fun, to let all guests give their two cents.

## Happy Travels

If you have many guests who live across the country or around the world, frame a map of the United States (or a world map) and have guests add a ball pin and a signature to the state or country in which they live. It is truly amazing to see how far your loved ones have traveled to attend your wedding! After the wedding, frame the map.

# The Card Box

Instead of a wrapped gift, many guests bring cards to a wedding. Rather than having to hand the card directly to the bride or groom, guests are often provided with a box in which to place them. This is also convenient for you, as it eliminates the possibility of misplacing cards in the midst of everything that is going on.

If you're going to have a card box, place it in a public area that guests won't miss, like on your guest-book table or cake table. Be sure to include a sign, so guests know that this is the spot they've been looking for. Have some crafty fun with it — print it on card stock from your computer, embroider or cross-stitch a sign and frame it, or spell out the word "Cards" in buttons.

As for the box itself, craft stores sell papier mâché boxes, which can be covered in fabric and embellished to coordinate with your wedding colors. Or, instead of a box, consider something a little more unexpected. Here are some ideas.

## Guitar Case

If you love to play music, use your guitar case as an impromptu card box. The same goes if you play the violin, saxophone, or any number of other instruments (though a cello case might be a bit overwhelming!).

## Luggage

Browse secondhand and antique shops for vintage luggage, perfect for keeping a lid on your wedding cards.

## Birdcage

Use a large, shabby-chic birdcage to house your cards, particularly if your wedding includes nature-inspired themes. Look for faux versions at craft stores, or search online or in antique stores for the real deal.

## Mailbox

I know of a bride who bought a wooden mailbox with her new last name burned into it. For her reception, she set it on a table, and guests opened the mailbox and placed their cards inside. After the wedding, they used the mailbox in their new home.

## Custom-Crafted Box

Can't quite find what you're looking for? Have a card box custom made! Search online, ask recently wedded friends for recommendations, or attend local craft shows or bridal shows to find an artisan who can create one for you.

# Table Numbers

Atable number doesn't have to be boring! Skip the traditional table numbers provided by your venue and create your own, using handcrafted ideas that correlate with your theme.

## Chalkboard Table Numbers

If your centerpiece utilizes potted plants, use miniature chalkboard signs with attached wooden stakes (available at FactoryDirectCraft.com). Write the table number on the chalkboard and insert the end of the stake firmly in the soil.

Create your own chalkboard place cards with ordinary picture frames. (Craft or dollar stores are excellent sources for inexpensive picture frames.) If the frame is unfinished or you want a different color, just use spray paint. Remove the picture-frame glass and apply chalkboard paint to it with a sponge brush. Allow the paint to dry overnight. If the glass is still visible, apply a second coat. After the paint is fully dry (24 hours is best), set the glass back into the frame and replace the backing. Now you can write the table number on the front with chalk or a chalk pen, which writes like a pen but dries (and erases) like chalk.

### Wine-Inspired Table Numbers

Wine bottles can be used in place of standard table numbers. The wine can be one that you and your sweetheart are fond of or perhaps a locally produced wine. Place a bottle on each table (along with a corkscrew and the directive to open and enjoy) and hang a table number from its neck. You'll help your guests find their tables and break the ice once they sit down.

For easy wine bottle chalkboard hangtags, use chalkboard signs (3-inch-square signs are available at FactoryDirectCraft.com or local craft stores). The signs come prestrung, and will fit easily over any wine bottle.

Create wooden hangtags by painting table numbers onto heart tags (available at craft stores). These tags are typically punched with a hole and can be tied with a length of natural twine. If you would prefer a less rustic look, replace the twine with a wide, double-faced satin ribbon.

### Flower Box Table Numbers

Combine your centerpiece and table number into one. Instead of a vase filled with flowers, use a wooden flower box. You can leave the wood unfinished or apply a coat of paint to complement your wedding palette. Purchase metal house numbers from a local home-supply store, and nail the appropriate numbers to each of the flower boxes. A nice idea would be to display the table number on both sides of the box, so guests can identify their table with ease.

### Book Table Numbers

Hardcover books can stand upright on their own when opened slightly, and they make unusual table numbers. Remove the dust jackets first, then use stencils, acrylic paint, and a sponge brush to stencil the table numbers onto the front covers of the books.

Alternatively, paint wooden numbers purchased from a craft store and attach them to the front covers with hot glue.

### Photo Table Numbers

Use heavy-duty card stock, stencils, paint, and a sponge brush to create table-number signs at home. Take photos of you and your groom holding each sign, then frame the photos and place them at the appropriate tables.

Another idea is to have each table number represent the bride and groom at a particular age; for instance, a sign at table 7 would include two photographs, one of the bride and one of the groom, both taken at age 7. Add taglines underneath to indicate memorable events for each year. This is a great opportunity to include your parents: ask them to contribute a memory or two for every photo. Be sure to make copies, so you don't ruin the originals!

## Wooden Table Numbers

Natural wood slices (available at www.Save-on-Crafts.com) — which are taken from fallen trees, not purposely cut down — become rustic table numbers with the use of a wood-burning tool. Simply inscribe the numbers on the slices and place them at the appropriate tables. To stand each slice upright, lean it against your centerpiece, or rest it on a small tabletop easel.

## Table Names

Rather than identifying tables by number, use names instead. Incorporate your love story into the names by including favorite places to visit, song titles, bands, or books. Include a small description underneath to tell guests why it is significant.

For instance, I attended a wedding where the couple worked their love for The Beatles into their wedding theme. Instead of being given numbers, each table was named after a Beatles song, like "Penny Lane" and "I Want to Hold Your Hand." As a fun way to break the ice for guests, the bride and groom included song lyrics at each table; guests were instructed to stand and serenade the couple in order to get them to kiss. The crowd enjoyed the interactivity; the couple enjoyed sharing their music with loved ones.

Instead of a song or particular band, name tables after your favorite flowers, or locations of some of your memorable dates. If you follow a certain sports team, name each table after a particular player you like.

Add these miniature canvas table numbers to your reception tables for color and a whimsical flair.

For this project, you'll need the following supplies:

- miniature canvases with matching-size easels
- a pencil
- hot-glue gun
- an assortment of buttons

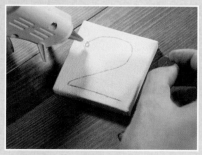

1. On the canvas, lightly draw the outline of the table number in pencil. Don't draw it too dark (canvas is not eraser friendly), just dark enough to use as a guide.

2. Beginning with one end of the number, place a small dab of glue out the beginning of your number on the canvas and press firmly.

3. Repeat this process, moving along button by button until the table number is complete.

4. Set the canvas on its easel.

# Escort Cards

Escort cards include a guest's name and his or her table assignment. These cards are typically placed near the entrance to the reception, so each guest can locate their card and find a seat at the appropriate table.

Escort cards are not mandatory, but are strongly recommended to ensure that guests have a reserved place to sit. If you use escort cards, guests will be more encouraged to mingle, because they won't waste time trying to find or save a seat. Escort cards make guests feel included.

### Farmhouse Charm

All sorts of rustic items can be used to help your guests find their seats. Use old window shutters to create an escort-card display by inserting the cards into its slats, or by clipping them on with mini clothespins.

Or, hammer rows of nails into the front of an old door and hang your escort-card tags from them.

### Pin Escort Cards

Make your escort cards into name tags. Using a 2½-inch-diameter paper punch, cut circles from decorative scrapbook paper, then write the names of your guests and their table assignments on each circle. Insert them into 2½-inch-diameter plastic-button pin blanks. Stick each pin into a folded tent card, and display them in alphabetical order on a table at the entrance to the reception area.

### Mason-Jar Escort Cards

What is one of the first things a guest does upon entering the reception? Grabs a drink! Give guests the opportunity to make a quick trip to the cocktail bar — and scope out seatmates — with a personalized Mason jar.

To craft escort jars, use blue painter's tape to mark off a rectangular area on the front of one-pint Mason jars. Coat that area with chalkboard paint (which can be purchased from any craft store) and let it dry. Peel off the tape, then write guests' names and table numbers on the chalkboard portion. Tie twine around the mouth of each jar, if you wish, as decoration.

A similar idea would be to customize wine or champagne flutes using wine charms personalized with each guest's name and table number. Buy wooden hearts from the craft store (a bag of five is about a dollar), along with ribbon and a fine-tip marker. On each heart, write a guest's name and his or her table assignment. Use a drill to make a hole at the top of the heart, thread ribbon through it, and tie it to the stem of a glass.

Arrange the jars or glasses in alphabetical order (or by table) for grab-and-go with ease. If you're using the jars, you might also want to offer colorful drinking straws, as many people aren't comfortable drinking directly from a Mason jar.

### *"Pick"-a-Table Escort Cards*

If you have a green thumb, consider an escort "flower box" that allows guests to "pick" their seat. Cut a piece of Styrofoam to fit into a decorative crate or large flower box. Glue artificial grass to the top of the Styrofoam. Cut out flowers from colorful construction paper, attach each to a length of floral wire, and wrap it with green floral tape. Glue a strip of paper with the guest's name and table number written on it to each flower. When finished, "plant" the flowers by sticking their wires into the Styrofoam. Guests pick their flower for their table assignment.

### *Luggage-Tag Escort Tags*

Create a travel-themed escort-card display with luggage tags and vintage suitcases (look for these at flea markets or estate sales). For the tags, write guests names and table assignments on shipping tags using a fine-point marker. Thread ribbon through the hole at the end of the tag. For the display, string several lengths of clothesline or twine across each open suitcase; secure the ends with a hammer and nails. Use clothespins to hang the tags from the clothesline. Display the suitcases on a table at the entrance to the reception.

### *Potted-Herb Escort Favors*

Create escort cards and favors in one fell swoop by using potted herbs. Purchase flats of herbs (like rosemary, basil, or thyme) from a garden center, 4-inch terra-cotta pots, potting soil, wooden plant-label sticks, and a fine-point permanent marker. Transfer each plant to a pot, filling in around it with moistened potting soil. Write the guest's name and table number on one side of the plant label; write the type of herb on the other side.

These pots look great as is, but with a little extra effort, you can incorporate some color. Before using them, sand the pots to remove imperfections, and wipe them down with a damp rag. Spray the inside of each pot with clear acrylic spray, then coat the outside with an exterior spray paint.

Apply a second coat of paint once the first dries; then apply a coat of clear acrylic to protect the paint.

Or, if you're artistic, use a silver or white metallic paint pen to draw designs; to add polka dots, lines, or zigzag patterns; or to simply write a guest's name on each pot. Best of all, after the festivities are over, the guests can take their herb-pot favors home.

### Personalized Mugs

You can order your own keepsake wedding coffee mugs from an online source like www.CafePress.com. Write each guest's name and table assignment on a length of ribbon with an acrylic marker and tie it to the handle.

Or, write each guest's name and table assignment on the front of a plain, white ceramic mug with an acrylic marker.

### Starfish Escort Cards

Planning a beach wedding? Turn starfish, seashells, or sand dollars into escort cards. Write the guest's name and table number on a length of ribbon with an acrylic marker and tie it around the beach loot of your choice.

### Soda Escort Cards

Greet guests with a refreshing twist: soda-bottle escort cards! Simply tie card stock tags to the top of each bottle. "Display" them on ice in a big galvanized washtub.

### Escort-Card Board

Print tent cards from your computer, or write them out by hand; also add a decorative monogram stamp to each card. Cover a 20 x 30-inch piece of foam board with lace or another decorative fabric (you'll need 3 yards), pulling it tightly across the board and securing it to the back with hot glue (and clothespins, until it dries). Pin the escort cards to the finished board, in alphabetical order, using pearlized, ball-head straight pins. Display the board on an easel at the entrance to the reception.

# Place Cards

While escort cards tell guests the table where they will be seated, place cards are set on every table, indicating a specific seat assignment for each guest. A place card also helps to acquaint guests. Create a simple place card using printable tent cards from an office-supply store. You can embellish the front of each printed card, if you wish, using craft-paper tape, lace ribbon, sequins, rhinestones, scrapbook stickers, or a stamp and ink pad. Use a bone folder to get a nice, sharp crease on each card.

I recommend printing the name of the guest on both sides of the place card, so seatmates across the table can address each other by name and avoid any gaffes.

### Doily Place Cards

Instead of using a tent card, write the guest's name in the center of a doily. You can do this yourself, using a black or gold marker; hire a calligrapher to do it; or print it using your computer (tape each doily to an 8 x 11-inch piece of paper, to make it easier to run it through the printer). Set the doilies on the guests' plates.

Alternatively, write or print the guest's name on a smaller-size doily, and use scissors to cut a slit into the bottom of the doily, less than half the way up. Insert the doily inside a mug, cup, or glass.

## *Pinwheel Place Cards*

Welcome guests to their table with a whimsical wedding idea: pinwheels! You can purchase pinwheels in bulk, attach a band of plain fabric to each and handwrite each guest's name. Or, order them customized and use your wedding colors and have them printed with each name.

## *Drink-Tag Place Cards*

In an effort to eliminate beverage confusion among your guests, create drink tags that can double as place cards. Print your guests' names on cardstock tags approximately 3 inches long and 1 inch wide. Once printed, use a hole punch at one end, then thread through a narrow ribbon. When guests arrive at their tables, they'll be greeted by a custom place-card drink tag, which they can tie around their wineglasses.

## *Bird-Nest Place Cards*

A bird-nest place card is a welcome twist to a traditional paper place card, particularly for bird-themed or springtime weddings. Use moss, decorative bird nests (available at craft stores), scissors, a fine-point marker, and card stock paper. Cut a tag from the paper (3½ inches long 1 inch wide), and write the guest's name with your marker. Place a small amount of moss inside each bird nest, lay the paper tag in the nest, and set the nest at each guest's seat.

## *Napkin-Ring Place Cards*

Craft easy place cards that double as napkin rings: just cut card stock into tags (4¾ inches long x 1 inch wide), write the guest's name on the tag, punch a hole at the side, and string raffia through it. Tie it around the guest's napkin.

Or, cut decorative scrapbook paper into strips approximately 6 inches long and 1 inch wide, and write the guest's name in the middle of the strip. Attach both ends of the paper together with double-sided tape, forming a ring around the napkin.

For a cute place card that ties into your table décor, consider this DIY idea which turns ordinary white handkerchiefs into beautiful handkerchief-flower place cards that tie effortlessly into your table setting.

These handkerchiefs — which I purchased for about five dollars for a set of twelve — create lovely flowers in a neutral palette of white, and are accompanied by an adorable button and nametag. If you're planning assigned seating at each table, tie a place card to a linen napkin at each guest's seat. Or, simply place them on the table.

## For this DIY project, you'll need to gather the following supplies:

- **handkerchiefs** (one per guest)
- **scissors**
- **pencil**
- **felt**
- **hot-glue gun**
- **needle and thread**
- **muslin fabric** (a piece 3½ inches long x ½ inch wide for each guest)
- **an alphabet stamp kit and ink pad**

1. First, let's make the flower. Place your handkerchief on a table and cut directly across the center; then, place one of the cut pieces on top of the other and cut once more. You will have four squares.

2. Place the squares in a pile and, using a pencil, trace the shape of a flower on the top very lightly.

3. Cut out the flower shape with your scissors, cutting through all layers at once.

4. Place the flower layers, one on top of the other, so the petal shapes are in random patterns. This will make the flower look more realistic.

5. Then, bunch the layers to create a floral bloom and sew the back of the flower to attach all layers together and hold the shape. If needed, use a dab or two of hot glue to create the look you want.

6. Take your muslin fabric and cut a small triangle from the side, to give the strip the appearance of a banner shape.

7. Stamp the guest's name on the muslin.

8. Use a dab of hot glue to add a button to the left side of the muslin fabric, next to the guest's name.

9. Use hot glue to adhere the muslin strip — with the button as the focal point and center portion of the flower — directly onto the handkerchief flower's center.

You can place a flower at each guest's place setting by wrapping it in ribbon and displaying it on a decorative plate.

Try using a piece of felt and a pin back to turn this floral idea into a place-card name tag or escort tag to be worn at the reception. This is also a fun idea for a garden-themed bridal shower and will help guests break the ice.

Instead of a white handkerchief, which I selected because I love the soft, thin material and how it offers a more formal look, feel free to select a more colorful handkerchief alternative instead. You can also roll up your sleeves and dye them yourself with fabric dye from the craft store. With a wide variety of colors available (in the intensity you desire, depending on how long they are placed in the dye), you'd be able to showcase a broad spectrum of hues with randomly picked flowers at each person's setting.

### Fruit Place Cards

Add whimsy and a punch of color to your tables by transforming seasonal fruit into place cards. Write guests' names on kraft tags, run a bit of twine through the tags, and attach them to the stems of bright red apples. Or write each guest's name in permanent marker on a miniature pumpkin. Or put a sunny yellow lemon at each guest's place setting with his or her name written on a decorative strip of paper that has been wrapped around the lemon and secured with tape.

### Stone Place Cards

Polished, black river rocks (found at home-supply stores) can be turned into place cards that your guests will want to take home. Write each guest's name on a stone with a metallic gold pen. Guests can then use the personalized stone as a paperweight, or can place it in their garden.

### Cork Place Cards

You can transform wine corks into place cards in a few easy steps. Cut each cork in half crosswise with an X-ACTO knife very carefully; sand the bottom of each with 60-grit sandpaper. Cut a slit into the top of the cork with the knife (if the slit is too thin, make a second cut to widen it). Write or print guests' names onto place cards (you can find them at office-supply stores); insert each card into the slit. Check eBay or your local craft store for purchasing wine corks in bulk.

### Charm Place Cards

A wineglass charm is a practical, inexpensive place card you can craft at home. Create small name tags from white cardstock and punch a hole on one side. Write the guest's name onto the tag. String metal wine-charm findings (available at craft stores) through the tag, to attach it to a wineglass stem. You can also use ribbons instead of the findings, but keep in mind that tying all those ribbons on the day of your wedding will be more time consuming.

### Floral Place Cards

A small vase becomes a floral favor and place card all in one! Fill a glass bud vase with water and set a single flower stem in it; write the guest's name on a paper tag, punch a hole, and tie the tag around the widest part of the vase with twine.

# Table Centerpieces

Centerpieces can be as simple or as elaborate as you wish, depending on your budget and level of expertise. Don't be afraid to call for assistance on this one: enlist the help of a friend who has an eye for decorating, or hire a florist. Florists work with brides on a regular basis and can often help brainstorm a perfectly pleasing centerpiece arrangement for your wedding day.

If you're willing to give it a go, roll up your sleeves and get inspired with these unique wedding-day centerpiece ideas.

## Mason-Jar

A Mason jar can incorporate a homespun look into nearly any décor. Cover the outside with lace, fabric, or burlap, tie a bow of twine or ribbon around it, fill it with water, and add a handpicked bouquet of wildflowers, baby's breath, or your favorite flower. Place a few jars at each table for a fuller look.

Or, instead of flowers, add a candle to a Mason jar for a romantic glow. For a twist, fill the jar with water and add a floating candle. Make sure any candles you use are kept

away from paper (obviously no one wants to be putting out fires on their wedding day). Also, use long-burning candles so, they don't go out during dinner.

You can create beach-themed centerpieces with Mason jars, by filling them with sand and adding seashells and/or sea glass. Or fill Mason jars with blue sea glass and dried glass plumes, and tie the jar with raffia.

### Candlelit Floral Wineglasses
Wineglasses can take on an entirely new function when set upside down. Place a silk flower in the center of each table, turn a wineglasses upside down directly over each one, and set a pillar candle on top.

### Planted Arrangements
Succulents placed in a decorative container (like a handmade or terra-cotta pot, or a teacup) can be paired with vintage books, framed photos, candles, or other visual accent pieces. After the wedding, invite guests to take the potted décor home as a favor.

### Vintage Cans
Old aluminum cans — washed, dried, and decorated — can be repurposed into centerpiece vases. Cover the cans with kraft paper, lace, fabric remnants, doilies, burlap . . . anything that coordinates with your décor. You can spray paint them for a bright pop of color, if you like — think aqua, green, or pink.

## Unconventional Candleholders

Candleholders can be made from materials you may not have considered. For instance, birch bark can be wrapped and hot glued around a glass votive candleholder, and placed on tables to tie into a woodland theme. Or, for soft candlelight, wrap a doily around a small glass jar or votive candleholder, and attach it with ribbon.

An ordinary glass candleholder also can be dressed up to tie into a beach-themed wedding. Glue small seashells to the holder, or coat the outside with rubber cement or another clear glue, and roll it in colored sand.

You can also cut a deep circle in the middle into of a squash, artichoke, apple, pear, or mini pumpkin to hold a votive or a tea-light candle.

## Themed Centerpieces

Consider a centerpiece that ties in directly with your wedding theme. For instance, a school-themed wedding could include a stack of books, a composition notebook, a set of pencils wrapped in twine, and a shiny red apple set on top; you could pair this with photo table numbers from the years that you and your fiancé were going to school. A book-themed wedding could incorporate a stack of hardcover books; for a bird-themed wedding, a birdhouse centerpiece set on a bed of moss would work perfectly. Finally, faux-passport place cards, framed-map table numbers, and globes as centerpieces would tie into a travel theme.

## Fruit

Fruit isn't just delicious; it's visually appealing, too. Lemons — naturally sunny and yellow — can be placed in an apothecary jar and used as a centerpiece suitable for spring or summer. Use oranges or limes instead if they work better with your color palette. For a fall wedding, apples or pears could be placed in small wooden boxes or baskets as centerpieces.

If you are using fruit, be sure to check out farmer's markets near you to support local agriculture!

### Picture Frames

Incorporate picture frames as your centerpiece, in addition to or instead of flowers. The frames can house memories of you and your soon-to-be spouse having fun in places you've traveled to or at some of your favorite hot spots around town. Include a caption so that guests can take something away from each image; who knows, maybe he or she will be inspired to check out that beautiful beachfront a few miles away, or choose a new travel destination as a result.

### Poetry

If you are a poet, or you love the work of a particular poet, have your favorite poems printed on card stock, then frame them and place them in the center of the table.

### Dessert Stands

Dessert can be used as a centerpiece; place macaroons, cupcakes, cookies, or tarts on a dessert stand set in the center of the table.

### Feathers

Instead of flowers, consider feathers. Feathers have the same colorful properties as flowers, but they don't wilt or require water. Feathers can add a glamorous look to any event when they are large, cascading, and set in a stylish vase. Incorporate crystal candlesticks to complete the look. Consider a black-and-white color palette, with white, feathery centerpieces that recall the glamour of the 1940s.

### Autumn Leaves

Gather colorful leaves, place them inside a large hurricane lamp, and top them with a battery-operated candle. You can also add pinecones (which you can spray paint or apply glitter to, if you like), acorns, or other natural objects. Another fall-themed idea would be to set a pillar candle atop a mound of moss and surround it with small vases of mums.

### Pinwheels

Pinwheels make a perfect alternative to flowers, particularly in the summer months. You can craft your pinwheels or buy them in your favorite colors. Place enough at each table in a vase for guests help themselves.

## *Sea Glass*

For a summer or destination wedding, incorporate sea glass into your décor. Fill a clear bowl or jar with sea glass (available in bulk at craft stores), or use it as a vase filler with a bouquet of flowers set on top.

## • TABLE RUNNERS •

Table runners add a textural element to your décor, while placing an emphasis on the centerpiece of your table.

### *Flowers*

If you love flowers, consider using most of your budget to create stunning floral runners. Arrange large bunches of your favorite blooms, like gerbera daisies, amaryllises, dahlias, hyacinths, orchids, or peonies, in short vases — nearly hidden by the blooms — along the center of your reception tables. This works particularly well if guests are seated at long, rectangular tables. For a budget-friendly alternative, consider using carnations. They've been given an undeserved bad rap — when used in bunches, they can make a powerful impact.

### *Linen*

Natural linen is so versatile. With its neutral tone, linen can tie into almost any color scheme and can be embellished any way you'd like. You can decorate a linen table runner with buttons or stencils and paint, or add lace trim to the ends with a needle and thread.

Leave the edges unfinished, or finish them with no-sew hem tape (by Dritz, found at any craft store). Simply fold the fabric back about half an inch on either side, apply the tape, and iron it to bond.

### *Lace*

Lace — purchased by the bolt — can be cut to size as a table runner. If white lace is too boring for your palette, add a little pep by dyeing it any shade under the sun.

Instead of using lace for a full-length table runner, you can place lace doilies under a vase centerpiece as a subtle — yet lovely — element.

### *Ribbon*

Use ribbons in complementing hues to create an unconventional and whimsical table runner. Simply arrange the strands next to one another from one side of the table to the other, draping them slightly over the sides of the table on each end. Or, sew or hot glue ribbon to linen, burlap, or lace table runners.

# Making a Wedding to Remember

With thoughtfully planned details and fun activities for guests, your wedding celebration will be the party to end all parties, one they'll remember long after the last song is played.

### Dance Lesson

Surprise guests with a fifteen- to twenty-minute ballroom or swing-dance lesson (either taught by you or a professional instructor) before the music gets started for the evening. It is a fun way to get guests out on the dance floor, it teaches them a new move or two, and it's a unique kickoff to the party.

For a Western-themed wedding, consider a line- or square-dancing lesson.

### Cigar Roller

If your groom and his buddies are cigar aficionados (and who knows, some of the ladies may be fans as well), hire a cigar roller who will roll cigars as you watch, for guests to take and enjoy. (Try www.CigarCatering.com for cities near you.)

### Karaoke

Invite guests to become wedding singers themselves with an open mic. Have your MC run the show for karaoke, and ask an outgoing friend to take the stage, to encourage other guests to do the same.

### Photo Booth

A photo booth is fun for guests and doubles as a take-home favor. For the do-it-yourself photo booth, provide a Polaroid instant camera, plenty of film, and LOTS of props (mustaches, chalkboards, picture frames, cowboy hats, boas, oversized sunglasses) to get them in the mood to say "cheese." Every photo booth requires a backdrop; outdoors, you can make your own by hanging a decorative sheet. For indoor venues, utilize a colorful wall or one with decorative wallpaper.

Encourage guests to take plenty of photos — some for them to take home, and others for guests to add to a wedding scrapbook that you can leave on a table nearby. This way, you'll have a wonderful, candid photo album cherish after the wedding.

Professional photo-booth companies are available for hire and can man the station, which makes it easy on you and your guests, since pros take care of the entire process. Typically, photographs taken in a professional photo booth are printed on photo strips, which can be placed inside a clear photo sleeve and taken home as a favor.

Create an area where guests can display their photos for the duration of the reception (before taking them home), and encourage guests to check them out throughout the festivities.

### A Preplanned Dance

Wow your guests with a preplanned dance, and set it to an up-tempo, crowd-pleasing song that will get everyone on their feet. Once you and your new husband enter the reception site, immediately take center stage and show off your dance number. Just be sure to practice it enough so that it goes off without a hitch.

### Lawn Games

If you're having an outdoor wedding, include a few popular games like horseshoes, croquet, a bean-bag toss, or bocce ball. Each of these games is a fun way for guests to pass the time — between the ceremony and reception, before dinner, after dinner, or for guests who don't like to dance.

### Make Everyone a Wedding Photographer

Make sure you get plenty of wedding antics caught on film by placing disposable cameras on all the tables. While you may have hired a stellar photographer, candid photographs taken of guests by guests will keep you laughing all the way to your honeymoon.

# Fun for the Kids

If you've ever attended a wedding as a kid, you know how boring it can be. There's no television, no video games, no games to play, nothing! If you're including kids at your wedding, make their mandatory attendance worth their while with a few activities they'll love. Who knows — your adult guests might enjoy them as well.

### A Magician

Hire a magician to come to the reception for a small block of time, to make balloon animals for the kids and perform a few magic tricks. Even better, ask the magician to teach the kids a trick or two they can do themselves. You can also arrange for the magician to take center stage after dinner and before dancing, for a short show that all the guests will enjoy.

### Coloring Books

At each of the kids' seats, place a coloring book and a box of crayons for them to color with. Activity books work great, too (with mazes, number games, and dot-to-dots worksheets), as they'll keep kids occupied a bit longer than coloring alone.

## • ESSENTIALS FOR GUESTS •

Your number-one concern for guests is their comfort. Keep them happy and smiling by anticipating their needs.

### For Mosquitoes

Outdoor weddings are beautiful; mosquito bites, however, are not. You can plan for bug bite prevention with a bug-spray station. Place a few bottles of repellent (look for the kind with a tolerable scent) in a basket and provide a sign telling guests to help themselves. They are more likely to enjoy the night — and stay longer — when not itching or swatting away those maddening mosquitoes.

### For the Loo

If you're having your wedding in the backyard, having 100 or more guests use one or two indoor bathrooms is a logistical nightmare, not to mention an incredible strain on any residential septic system. So be sure to provide portable outdoor bathrooms — call them port-o-johns or port-o-sans (I prefer outdoor loo). For your guests' comfort, be sure to tailor the number you rent to the number of guests — you don't want your grandmother waiting in a line six deep. And these days, there are many options for portable bathrooms, including ones that are essentially trailers with multiple stalls, lights, and sinks. Whatever your budget, you should be able to find an option to fit it.

If you end up opting for the classic port-o-john, here are some suggestions for making it, shall we say, a little more civilized.

Most females run to the bathroom to check their hair or makeup or to fix their dress. Provide a mirror somewhere, whether it be inside the loo hanging on the door, or nearby — possibly a full-length mirror propped against a tree.

Be sure to stock plenty of antibacterial hand soap and a lavender-scented air freshener.

Also, it's important to install appropriate lighting once the sun goes down. Torches placed outside the bathrooms will help your guests find the way there. Battery-operated lanterns inside the bathrooms are your best choice. If space is an issue, get those push lights that require a few batteries in the back. Add a strip of adhesive and mount them on the wall inside.

Finally, position a basket full of help-yourself goodies on a table located near the bathrooms — antibacterial wipes, a bottle of aspirin, toothpicks, gum or mints, combs, feminine products, tissues, safety pins, and more. This one-stop station will definitely give guests the comfort of indoor plumbing while enjoying the rustic atmosphere of your wedding site.

### For Heat and Humidity

If you're getting married outdoors during the summer months, supply your guests with paper fans — distributed before the ceremony — or a basket of battery-operated fans placed nearby to help them keep cool.

### For Raindrops

You can't stop rain from falling, but you can keep your great-aunt from getting soaked while waiting for you to walk down the aisle. If you're having an outdoor wedding, it's a good idea to have plenty of umbrellas on hand. And remember, rain on your wedding day is a sign of good luck.

### For Sore Feet

To combat achy feet and prevent those dancing mamas from skipping out on the hustle, provide a basket of inexpensive flip-flops in a variety of sizes (a few 7s, 8s, 9s, 10s, and, for other tall ladies like me, an 11 or two). For only a few bucks a pair, you'll save guests from dancing in bare feet or skipping the dance floor altogether. I've heard of ladies stepping on broken glass while dancing barefoot. Yikes. Protect those feet, ladies!

### For Chilly Weather

At an outdoor wedding, once the sun goes down, it is bound to get a little bit chilly. Give the gift of warmth by furnishing the ladies with a basket of shawls (in your wedding colors, if possible) to borrow.

# CHAPTER 6

# Food and Drink

—◇—

If I had to select two areas of a wedding that guests love most, I'd say it is the food and drink. In this chapter, I'll show you how to put a personal twist on these two crowd-pleasers.

# Food

**B**rides, remember that guests pay close attention to the food and drink. Don't let this part of your wedding planning fall off your to-do list: be sure to create a memorable wedding menu!

### Themed Menus

Consider a menu based on the theme of your wedding. For instance, if you are planning a backyard wedding, complete with gingham tablecloths and lawn games, serve home-style family favorites like barbecued chicken, hamburgers, pasta salad, and corn on the cob, with cherry pie for dessert.

Planning by season? An autumnal wedding menu could include turkey, stuffing, mashed potatoes, and cranberry sauce, followed by pumpkin pie.

Beach wedding-goers dive into a seafood selection of shrimp cocktail and grilled salmon or tuna, served with fresh lemon wedges. For dessert, offer Key lime pie instead of traditional cake, and send guests home with sugar cookies in seaside or nautical shapes (like starfish or sailboats) as favors.

Carnival-themed weddings require festive fare. Serve up corn dogs and cotton candy, packaged in monogrammed wrappings to make them your own.

Planning a Cinco de Mayo wedding? Offer mini tacos, enchiladas, or burritos for cocktail fare . . . and don't forget the margaritas.

Southern-themed weddings deserve the honest-to-goodness flavor of Southern cooking, like shrimp and grits, fried chicken, and corn bread, served with sweet tea and lemonade in Mason jars.

If you're planning a 1950s theme complete with cheeseburgers, french fries, and juke-box tunes, whip up a do-it-yourself milk-shake station with striped straws, large stir spoons, whipped cream, and Maraschino cherries.

## Favorite Foods and Hobbies

Instead of planning by theme, why not create a menu centered on your favorite foods, or one that ties into your hobbies? If your groom's idea of a perfect vacation involves fishing, make fish the main course. If you are an expert in gardening, make sure there's plenty of fresh garden greens and other vegetables on the menu. Love stir-fries? Find a chef to make this your main menu item. (You'd be surprised how many restaurants will do off-site catering.)

## Breakfast, Brunch, or Lunch

If a dinner menu isn't what you had in mind for your wedding, serve another meal instead. Following a morning wedding, you can opt for breakfast or brunch. Offer up scrambled eggs, made-to-order omelettes, pancakes, French toast, waffles, fruit, oatmeal, bacon, sausage, bagels, and all the fixings.

A luncheon, served after noon, is another option, featuring soup, light sandwiches, pasta salads, and fruit.

# Cake

Your wedding cake doesn't have to be a particular size, flavor, or style; technically, it doesn't even have to be a cake at all. Your wedding cake can be anything you dream of, as long as it tastes as good as it looks.

## Traditional Wedding Cake

Wedding cake typically consists of layers, filling, and icing. The layers can include anything you love, from cherry-nut, to red velvet, to devil's food. The filling can be a traditional flavor like chocolate, vanilla, raspberry, or lemon, or a specialty filling like pecan, chocolate mousse, or cream cheese. Finally, you have the icing — the best part, I think — which covers the surface of the cake and can include buttercream, fondant, whipped cream, or ganache.

If you're unsure where to begin, consider a few popular cake choices according to the season. In the winter, a romantic red-velvet cake with cream-cheese filling or a spice cake with buttercream are rich options, while a lighter white cake with lemon or raspberry filling (or a beachy vanilla sponge cake with a tropical-fruit or coconut filling) fits in nicely with a spring or summer wedding.

The best advice for cake flavors and fillings is to give them a try. Visit a local bakery for a cake tasting. It's a free, fun date with your fiancé, and it can help tremendously in your quest for the perfect cake.

## The Handcrafted Cake

If you are a great baker and you're ready to take it to the next level, you can bake your own cake. However, do your homework: pick a recipe and bake a few trial cakes before the big day. Once you feel confident in your ability, make a schedule a few days before the wedding for baking, frosting, and chilling your cake in the refrigerator. Also, figure out how your cake will be transported to the wedding reception and where it will be stored prior to being cut. Baking your own cake can be stressful, but in the end you will feel satisfied in having it done the way you want it.

## Decorate Your Cake

How your cake is decorated is another way you and your fiancé can express yourselves on your wedding day. Here are some ideas to get you started.

## Rainbow Colors

Surprise guests with colorful layers — just add food coloring! A rainbow wedding cake — with multiple colorful layers — can be covered in white frosting. Imagine your guests' reaction when you cut into the cake to reveal every color of the rainbow! Or decorate the exterior of the cake with a thick coating of rainbow sprinkles, or using different colors of candies (like Nerds, Skittles, or M&Ms) on each layer.

Alternatively, use just two shades on alternating layers; or, go for an ombré look and select one shade, with each layer a slightly darker intensity.

### Stripped Back and Structural
Or, skip the frosting altogether for a "naked" look, revealing only layers and fillings. Use a cake batter that screams celebration, like Funfetti (by Pillsbury), which has specks of edible confetti throughout.

### Delightful Details
A traditional wedding cake can be more memorable with unexpected embellishments. Drape the tiers with cascading fondant flowers, add edible candy pearls (in white, silver, or gold), or apply a ribbon trim to the bottom of the tiers, removed prior to serving.

### Crazy for Dots
Add color and whimsy to the exterior of your cake with polka dots made from fondant. Just roll out the fondant, use a cookie cutter or round cap in the size you want to cut them out, and drape them on the cake.

### Themed Decoration
For a nature-inspired wedding cake, decorate it with fondant leaves or sugary faux pinecones. Or cover it with fondant fashioned to look like birch bark, with fondant "twigs" decorating the tops of the tiers. Set the cake on a wooden-slab cake stand.

A beach wedding cake can be adorned with edible chocolate-filled seashells or hard-candy sea glass (available at www.SeaGlassCandybyMarcia.com) placed along the tiers. Lightly coat the cake in brown sugar for the illusion of sand, or cover it with light-blue icing, and add seashells or starfish cut from fondant or piped on in another color of icing, so that they cascade down the tiers.

## • CAKE ALTERNATIVES •

You've heard "let them eat cake," but who says the cake part is mandatory? Consider these alternatives to the traditional wedding cake.

### Cupcakes
Cupcakes are a fun alternative to wedding cake, because you can customize the designs on the tops, the wrapper colors, and the sizes. Since they are already in individual servings, you can skip the cake-cutting fee most venues charge.

Cupcakes can also function as a table centerpiece. Just place cupcakes (one for each guest at the table) on a two- or three-tiered cupcake tower in the middle of each table.

### Pavlova

This is a light, meringue-based dessert topped with whipped cream and fruit. It is a perfect summertime dessert and can be placed on cake stands with different fruit options for each. My favorite is chocolate raspberry pavlova — yum!

### Rice Krispies Cake

It's the Rice Krispies treat to end all Rice Krispies treats! Serve up a tiered Rice Krispies "cake" using graduated sizes of cake pans. If you like, add food coloring to the marshmallow mix before mixing it with the cereal for a more colorful "cake."

### Cookie Cake

Stacked cookies — like Oreos, sugar cookies, or gingerbread — can combine the look of a wedding cake with the fun of a cookie bar. No cake needed — just stack the cookies to form a "cake," and instruct guests to take from the top to avoid a collapse. Serve with milk!

### Cake Pops

Cake pops are made by baking a cake, allowing it to cool, then crumbling it, mixing it with frosting, and rolling the mixture into balls. Insert lollipop sticks (available at Jo-Ann stores) and you've got cake pops. You can then gild the lily by coating the pops with sprinkles, crushed candy, melted chocolate, caramel, or more frosting.

To create a display for them, take a decorative box and cut a piece of Styrofoam to fit inside it. Cover the top of it with billows of Easter grass, then insert the cake pops into the Styrofoam for guests to grab and go.

### Donuts

Skip the cake and opt for dozens of sugary donuts instead, stacked on tiered cake stands.

### Brownie Cake

Use brownie batter instead of cake batter to create a brownie wedding cake, separated by layers of frosting.

## Pie

I remember a wedding where the bride asked her aunts to bake pies for her reception. They used family recipes handed down from the bride's grandmother and baked up apple, cherry, peach, and pecan pies. It was a nice way for the bride to pay homage to her grandmother.

You can replicate this idea by baking up a few of your favorite pies — or asking a friend to help — and setting them on cake stands of varying heights. Include signs indicating the pie flavors (and be sure to mention if the pies were made by a special family member or friend).

You could also make flavor flags for the pies. Cut 2-inch-long flags from a piece of muslin; using an alphabet stamp set, stamp the flags with the flavors of the pies. Use a hot-glue gun to attach each flag to a toothpick. Insert them in the pies.

## Ice Cream

If you're not interested in cake in any way, order up ice cream instead! A do-it-yourself ice-cream bar is a fun way for guests to get involved. Kids really love it. Offer guests plenty of flavors to choose from, and don't skimp on toppings. They can include fresh fruit, nuts, hot-fudge sauce, caramel, whipped cream, gummy bears, sprinkles, and, of course, Maraschino cherries for the cherry on top! Be sure to have waffle bowls, cones, and spoons available — and napkins.

An alternative is to cool off your guests with ice cream in a jar. Buy your favorite flavor of ice cream and place a few scoops in each jar. Add a topping or two if you'd like, close the lid, affix a label, and tie a ribbon with a miniature spoon attached. Be sure to check with your reception site to make sure that they have enough room in their freezer to make this idea feasible.

## Waffles

A waffle bar makes a delicious dessert alternative when presented with toppings like whipped cream, fresh strawberries, blueberries, and a choice of fruit and maple syrups.

## Cheese

Wine-loving couples, take notice: you can pair a wine-themed wedding with a final cheese course instead of a wedding cake, served up with a selection of appropriate wines.

## • THE CAKE TOPPER •

Whether your cake is large, small, or not a cake at all, wedding cakes need a topper. Toppers range from a single initial or monogram to custom-ordered bride-and-groom bobbleheads.

### Floral Cake Topper

Using flowers as a cake topper is a simple and stylish option. Keep the flowers fresh in water up until the reception begins, then have them placed on the cake. I've seen this done with hydrangeas, peonies, lilies, and daisies (particularly gerbera daisies, since they are available in plenty of color choices).

### Hand-Painted Cake Topper

If you've browsed the bride-and-groom toppers but can't find one that fits you, make your own. From a craft store, purchase blank wooden figurines with a circle for a head and a solid-wood body. This allows you to paint in the face and clothes just the way you want to — wearing jerseys from your favorite sports team, college gear, or whatever you like, to showcase your interests or part of your love story.

### Heart Cake Topper

Buy a wooden heart charm and dowel from a craft store. Paint the heart to match your color palette, use a wood-burning tool to "carve" your initials in it, or cover the heart in a pretty fabric. Attach the heart to the dowel with wood glue and let it dry overnight. Once it's ready, stick it into the top tier of your cake and enjoy.

You can skip the wood altogether, and create a fabric heart topper by sewing a heart from linen, stuffing it with polyfill, and then sewing it closed. Attach it to the dowel.

## Vintage Cake Topper

A cake topper from a previous decade may be the style for you. If you don't mind rummaging through thrift stores or shopping online, you're likely to find one you love. Better yet, borrow the cake topper your parents or grandparents used at their wedding. If you're planning to serve several cakes, a fun idea would be to display your topper as well as those of your parents, your in-laws-to-be, and your grandparents (yours and his). Be sure to place yours on the cake you'll be cutting.

## Photographic Monogram

Create a simple cake topper using wooden letters, two wooden sticks, and hot glue. Glue the letters to the tops of the sticks; allow them to dry overnight. Decorate the monogram with photographs traced and cut out to fit on the letters; attach them with hot glue. Stick the base of the sticks into the cake.

## Bird Toppers

Lovebirds, this one's for you! Reflect your bird theme by adding birds to your cake. Here are a few ideas to inspire you.

Create a cake topper with wooden bird decoys from a craft store. Add paint for decoration, use hot glue to attach them to wooden sticks (don't paint the sticks, to keep them food safe), and insert them in the cake.

Arrange decorative bird nests from a craft store on your cake. Add reindeer moss and Jordan almonds (to look like bird eggs), and place small, wooden-letter initials inside as your monogram.

## Cupcake Flags

You can dress up your cupcakes with flags. To make them, print out the words or phrases you'd like to include on your toppers, like the date of your wedding, "Forever," "Just Married," "Love," "Laughter," or "Joy." You can also add a monogram to each one. Cut the messages out and paste them onto fabric cut into small banners or flags, and attach them to toothpicks with a dab of glue. Insert the flags into the cupcakes.

## • THE CAKE SERVER •

My venue offered cake cutting and a server rental, but I wanted to make and use my own. I found an inexpensive cake server at a craft store, purchased small rhinestone crystals, and hot glued them to the handle. Then I tied a coordinating ribbon around the handle.

You can do what I did to make an ordinary cake server something special, or you can borrow one, or buy a silver set and have it engraved. It's not a bad investment; you'll need a cake server in your home, and it becomes a keepsake when it has your own unique stamp on it.

## • CAKE STANDS •

Cake stands make dessert-table setups a breeze. You can buy them new, search for vintage cake stands, or make your own. You can also add embellishments to your cake stands. Check out craft stores for ribbon, crystal teardrops, or another decoration to hook onto each stand.

### Rustic Wedding Stand

A rustic wedding theme requires a cake stand that follows suit. Consider a tiered, wooden cake stand or a single "slice" from a tree trunk. Carve your initials into the top with a wood-burning tool for added personalization.

I couldn't believe how easy it was to make my own cake stand; now, every time I visit a thrift store, I am on the lookout for decorative plates I can transform into a cake or dessert stand. This makes a great display piece for desserts, either on your cake table or at individual tables as centerpieces. Be careful when transporting it, carry the cake stand underneath the base, never lifting from a plate directly.

### For this project, you'll need the following supplies:

- two decorative plates, any size
- newspaper
- hot-glue gun
- one 2-3 inch tall glass candlestick
- one 4-5 inch tall glass candlestick

1. Place one of the plates, top side down, on newspaper. Apply hot glue to the top of the smaller candlestick and press it firmly into the plate. Allow to dry.

2. Repeat step one, but take the taller candlestick and hot glue the top of it to the bottom of the second plate, this is the second tier. Allow to dry.

3. Once dry, dab hot glue around the bottom of the taller candlestick.

4. Adhere the taller candlestick to the center of the first plate as shown in the photograph. Allow to thoroughly dry overnight.

# Drinks

Make an impression on guests by offering a custom drink menu. Here are some ideas to get you started, including plenty of handcrafted drink accessories.

## *Signature Drink*

If you have a favorite drink, consider serving it at your reception — a family favorite, like your mom's special homemade iced tea, or a punch, housed in a large glass beverage dispenser or a punch bowl. Add a label to the front and a ribbon for decoration, with glasses nearby and ice, if appropriate.

If you're serving a special drink, give it a new name. For instance, you could label drink dispensers filled with iced tea or a punch something like "Love Potion" or "Sweet-Love Sangria." Serve a drink at the bar like a "Marry Me Martini" or "Grin and Tonic." Beer bottles can have custom labels affixed to them that read, "Ale You Need Is Love," "I-Do Brew," or "Veil Ale." Use your imagination to create a custom label suited to your special occasion.

## Champagne

When guests arrive at the reception, greet them with miniature champagne bottles ready for toasting. You can order these from Korbel (www.korbel.com) or buy them in bulk from a local liquor store. Place the bottles in small bowls filled with ice to keep them chilled. Prior to your guests' arrival, have a designated person pop the mini bottles. Make sure to have straws on hand for sipping.

## Home Brew

If your groom or a family member brews beer at home, have a special blend made for the wedding day. To serve it to all guests, you'd need a large-quantity batch; or, keep it simple by crafting beer in special bottles just for the bridal party. Add a custom label.

## Wine

The same idea can be applied to wine, if a family member makes his or her own. You could request a special blend made just for your wedding, with a custom label (noting the family member, of course, who created the delicious wine). Then, give the wine to guests as gifts, or serve it up as a specialty drink at the bar. It's a nice way to pay homage to the family member's talent, while providing the best compliment you could — offering it to your guests!

For a wine-themed wedding or one held at a winery, arrange for a wine tasting in lieu of cocktails. Give guests wineglass favors to use through the night and to take home to commemorate the wedding. Out-of-town guests can tour the local wineries the next day.

## Specialty Bar

Feature a specialty bar at your wedding. (You can do this with alcoholic or nonalcoholic beverages.)

A cigar-and-brandy bar would be a hit for the gentlemen in your party and could tie into a Casino Night theme. A martini bar would work as well. Extra olives, please.

Plan a coffee bar, complete with different flavors of your favorite blends, specialty creams, and toppings like marshmallows, whipped cream, and chocolate shavings, served up in decorative glassware (or take-home cups to go). Hire someone to keep the toppings stocked and the coffee fresh and piping hot.

## Colorful Drinks

Planning a wedding with bursts of sunny yellow? Serve lemonade, lemons-drop cocktails, or limoncello collinses (gin, limoncello, lemon juice, and club soda). For a lime-green event, offer mint juleps or iced green tea. A pretty-in-pink theme calls for pink-grapefruit mojitos, rosé wine, or pink lemonade.

## Soda

For a fun nonalcoholic option, serve up some old-fashioned favorites like root beer or black cherry, grape, or cream soda in glass bottles. Place the bottles in a large tub of ice to stay cold, or have them on hand at the bar.

## Plenty of $H^2O$

If your wedding is held outdoors (particularly in hot or humid weather), providing water bottles for guests is a great idea. Apply a custom wedding label (available at www.myownlabels.com) and place them in a large cooler. Include a sign for guests to help themselves, along with a recycling receptacle nearby.

## Fruit

Lemonade is even more appealing with slices of fresh lemon, lime, or orange, or with handfuls of raspberries, blackberries, or blueberries added to it. Have fruit on hand for guests to add themselves, or place it inside a large glass container to dress up a signature drink.

## Drink Stirrers

Create spirited drink stirrers with easily found wooden craft sticks and small hearts. Use a dab of hot-glue to attach the wooden heart to the top of the craft stick and then write (with an oil-based Sharpie marker) your initials or emblem of your wedding on the heart. Place the stirrers in a cup at the bar for your guests to use.

Flag drink stirrers are whimsical and require only cotton fabric, scissors, and wooden stir sticks (7 inches long). Cut a strip of fabric (2 inches long x 1 inch wide) and attach it to one end of a stir stick with a knot. Use the same solid color for all flags, or mix it up with a rainbow of colors and patterns. (Packets of remnant squares will save you money.)

Consider a novelty drink stirrer for the occasion. Miniature umbrellas placed in drinks could fit with an island-themed wedding. For the holidays, glue a gold or silver pom-pom (or tinsel) atop a wooden stir stick to add instant glam to any drink.

Chocolate- or coffee-loving couples could use chocolate spoons — available at specialty-chocolate or gourmet shops — for guests to stir their coffee or hot chocolate. These spoons are sold in a range of gourmet flavors, including hazelnut and Irish cream.

Use candy as drink stirrers: consider lollipops, licorice, rock-candy sticks, or old-fashioned striped candy sticks. Drink stirrers with a specialty flavor built right in — like apple martini — can be purchased in bulk from www.Candy.com.

A holiday or season can inspire unexpected drink customization. Use candy canes as stir sticks for the holidays, or create a custom drink by dipping glass rims into melted chocolate, then crushed peppermint, and letting it harden. In the fall, serve hot apple cider with cinnamon sticks as stirrers.

Dress up drinks with polka-dotted or striped straws in fun, punchy colors from www. ShopSweetLulu.com.

Personalize swizzle sticks with your names, wedding monogram, or logo at www. ForYourParty.com, which offers stir sticks printed on eco-friendly wood, and a sizable selection of fonts and colors.

### Custom Coasters

If you plan on serving your own specialty drink, consider printing the name of it and your wedding monogram onto coasters. You can order them from a specialty printing company or a restaurant-supply store. Place them on tables, or at the bar for guests to grab.

### Cocktail Napkins

For easy, customized cocktail napkins, buy napkins in your wedding colors and add your monogram with a stamp and archival ink.

# CHAPTER 7
# Wedding Favors

◄◦►

Say good-bye to wedding favors that guests will never use, never remember where they came from, and, worst of all, never keep. A custom that was created as a way to say thank you to guests has become cheap and impersonal. Where is the love?

The love can be found in homespun, handcrafted favors that have been created with your guests in mind. Select a wedding favor that reflects you as a couple, to give as a token of your sincere appreciation.

# Culinary Favors

Edible favors are always a hit; everyone loves food, and once it's gone . . . it's gone! No holding onto a wedding favor for months afterward or feeling too guilty to throw it away. Guests who are hungry before dinner can enjoy the favor right away, while others might take it to go. Here are some delicious ideas.

### Homemade Jam and Other Preserves and Savories

Whip up a jar of your own delicious strawberry, raspberry, blueberry, or peach jam, place a label on the front, and tie a ribbon around the lid. Spiced peaches, pickles, and marinated olives are other tasty choices. If making your own is too much of an undertaking, there are plenty of gourmet products available for purchase. Just add a ribbon and a thank-you tag.

### Cookies

If you've always wanted to have your own bakery, how about offering a to-go cookie buffet? I recommend including at least six kinds of cookies in pretty glass jars, so guests have plenty of options. Make cookie catching easier with a pair of tongs in each container, along with a card telling guests what's inside (which helps guests with allergies). If you know you will have guests who are vegans and/or celiacs, it would be very thoughtful to include at least one kind of cookie for them.

Make cookies even sweeter with personalization: bake up sugar cookies, cut them out using your monogram.

If you're famous for your chocolate-chip cookies, bake up several batches right before the wedding, and send them home with guests in custom packages. A paper CD sleeve is the perfect size to be used as a takeaway container for a cookie. Order custom stickers to place on the front (or print your own off the computer), and it's done! Colored cellophane bags tied with a ribbon are another option.

For a punch of color, wrap individual cookies in waxed paper and seal with tape. Then wrap each cookie — as though you were wrapping it as a present — in colorful tissue paper, adding a ribbon embellishment.

For an added personal touch, include the recipe along with the cookie in the package. Or you could tie a cookie cutter onto each one. They are available in so many shapes that you can likely find one to fit in with your theme, like a snowflake for a winter wedding, or you can always go with the classic heart shape.

For added charm, offer cartons (like you bought in the cafeteria at grade school) or glass bottles of milk for guests to take an old-fashioned milk-and-cookie break. I've even seen milk served up in fancy glasses for a more glorified dipping experience. You're never too old for milk and cookies!

### Cookie Mix in a Jar
If the idea of baking hundreds cookies for guests sounds like too big a task, consider cookie mix in a jar. The dry ingredients needed to make the cookies can be placed in a Mason jar, with an attached recipe instruction sheet. Create your own custom label for the front of the jar, and add fabric with clear elastic to decorate the lid.

You can incorporate a wooden spoon into the favor, attaching it to the side of the jar with twine. On the spoon's handle, use a wood-burning tool to engrave a message (like "We love you" or "Thank you"), or write their family name on it.

### Fortune Cookies
Bring good fortune to guests with custom fortune cookies. You can order them online (www.myluckyfortune.com) with your own personal message inside! Share a favorite short quote, words of wisdom, or say thank you in your own words.

### Honey in a Jar

Give small jars of honey as favors. One of my favorite sources is Hillside Bees, based in New Hampshire. This team of beekeepers offers small jars of honey, wrapped with a ribbon and paired with a wooden dipper ready for gifting. Go to www.etsy.com/shop/HillsideBees and look for their honey wedding favors.

### S'mores

Get back to your Girl Scout self and offer a s'mores buffet. This can be set up indoors using chafing-dish candles (and caution, obviously) to roast marshmallows on skewers. On a table, arrange the skewers with marshmallows alongside the lit candles (set on plates, of course), immediately followed by graham crackers and chocolate bars. Place glassine bags at the end of the buffet for transporting them to go, as well as plates for guests to savor them immediately. Check with your reception venue in advance, to make sure they're okay with this idea.

Love the idea but want to skip the skewers? Pack mini s'more favors to go, with two graham crackers, two marshmallows, and a chocolate bar in a decorative bag.

### Cupcakes

Offer plain cupcakes, frostings, and toppings on a table for guests to build their own cupcakes. If you want to offer guests the option to take their cakes home, and leave them for guests to grab on the go.

### Caramel Apples

Perfect for autumn weddings, this idea offers guests the opportunity to dress up a yummy apple with delectable toppings. On a buffet table, place apples on skewers alongside chafing dishes or small slow cookers filled with warm caramel, hot-fudge sauce, and/or white chocolate. Have plenty of chopped nuts, crushed candies and candy bars, sprinkles, and chocolate chips available for additional topping options. Make sure to provide clear bags and ties for guests to take their apples to go.

### Lollipops

Make your own lollipops using a thematic mold (butterflies, hearts, your initials), then wrap them in cellophane and secure them with a pretty bow.

### Mini Pies

Bake small pies — or buy them from a favorite bakery — and place them inside small cardboard boxes secured with baker's twine. Attach a plastic fork with a "thank you" card to each.

### Candy

A to-go candy buffet can be a visual knockout, but without proper planning, you run the risk of it looking sparse. I recommend purchasing at least eight to ten different candies at one quarter to one half a pound per guest. I know, that's kind of an amazing amount, but you want to ensure that the buffet is stocked so well that guests won't feel like the "good stuff" is all gone too soon.

For a perfect candy buffet, buy or rent glass containers like large vases, punch bowls, and apothecary jars to house each type of candy. It is important to affix an identifying label on the front of each, which can be made from decorative card stock secured with a satin ribbon. Include candy scoops to discourage guests from digging in with their hands, and don't forget the old-fashioned paper bags complete with a handle, just like the candy shop offered when you were a kid. Stamp your monogram on the front of each bag for a personal touch. And be sure to visit the buffet throughout the night yourself . . . after all the hard work, you've earned the right to indulge your sweet tooth.

### Local/Family Favorites

Is your town or region noted for its saltwater taffy, maple syrup, or a particular fruit? Does someone in your family have culinary specialty that is transportable? Look for mini offerings of these products or, if appropriate, buy them in bulk and then use them to fill custom favor bags.

### Chocolate

The favors at our wedding were chocolate bars packaged in wrappings that coordinated with our décor. Think about adding a custom label to your favorite candy bar or wrapping it in fabric. Skip this idea for a summer wedding, since no one likes melted chocolate!

### Cider and Donuts

Coordinate the season with the favor. In the fall, send guests home with cider and donuts. Buy local cider, pour it into glass jars, add a custom label (including the name of the local mill it came from), and offer it along with donut holes in a sweet kraft-paper bag with a custom stamp. Be sure to keep the cider refrigerated right up until the time of the wedding.

### From the Farm

Consider creating a miniature farmer's market with bushels of apples or peaches, along with small paper bags to fill, or with mini baskets of cherries, blueberries, raspberries, or strawberries. Make sure you include a wooden sign that reads, "Please Pick Your Own!"

Or, place two pears in a small burlap bag tied with ribbon, along with a tag that reads, "The Perfect Pair."

## Trail Mix

Fill various containers to the brim with good stuff like granola, raisins, dried cranberries and blueberries, chocolate chips, sunflower seeds, and nuts of all kinds. Have scoops on hand along with individual bags for guests to fill, all of them labeled "For the Trail."

A sweet favor for tea-lovers, one that will warm their heart and soul. perfect for autumn or winter weddings.

---

For this project, you'll need the following supplies for each favor:

- **two tea bags** (Generic green or black tea will do.)
- **scissors**
- **felt**
- **hot-glue gun**
- **a drawstring cloth spice bag**
- **small (1-inch) wooden heart**
- **alphabet stamp kit and ink pad**
- **vintage teacup saucer** (Look for these in thrift stores and at estate and garage sales.)

1. Remove each tea bag from its outer paper wrap.

2. Cut out hearts from the felt, being careful to make them the same size. You'll need four hearts per favor, as each tea bag will require two hearts (per string).

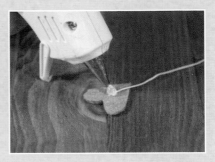

3. Place one heart on the table, apply a dab of hot glue, and attach one side of the tea-bag string to the heart. Then place the second heart on top of the first. Press firmly.

4. Follow the same procedure for the second bag of tea.

5. Place both tea bags inside the spice bag, with the heart tags hanging on the outside.

6. On the wooden heart, stamp "Tea for Two."

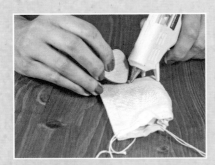

7. Hot glue the wooden heart to the outside of the spice bag.

8. Place the tea favor on the saucer, and place it at each guest's table setting.

# Keepsake Favors

When giving a favor to guests, consider functionality as well as individuality. Tie these two elements together, and guests will hold onto your favor long after the wedding day.

## Book of Recipes

My mom and sister included a blank recipe card with my bridal-shower invitations, asking guests to contribute a favorite recipe to a recipe book at the shower. As a result, I have a collection of the most delicious passed-down recipes from my family and friends; each recipe card is handwritten, with helpful hints about how he or she perfected the recipe over time or why it is his or her favorite. My recipe book is one of my most cherished gifts, one that I reference on a regular basis. Give guests a similar gift by including a handmade booklet of your and your spouse-to-be's favorite recipes, printed from your computer and finished with a patterned paper cover (made from scrapbook paper or card stock).

## Pencils

There are few things sweeter in autumn than falling leaves, apple cider, donuts, and freshly sharpened pencils for the first day of school. If you're planning a wedding with a school theme, consider this favor: create a kraft tag with your monogram or "thank you" stamped onto the front. Punch a hole on the side and string twine through it. Wrap the twine around a pack of five no. 2 pencils (personalized with a fine-tip marker, or ordered from an online source) and place it at each setting, along with a place-card apple (see page 118).

## Wedding CD or DVD

Keep guests singing along to your handpicked wedding playlist with a CD. Order personalized CD stickers from a print service (like www.Beau-Coup.com) that include your names, the wedding date, and track listings. Or, before the wedding, compile a thank-you video to tell guests what their attendance at your wedding means to you. The video should be short and sweet (a minute or two in length) and completely heartfelt. Gift the video as a DVD for guests to watch after the wedding.

## Succulent Favors

A succulent is a long-lived, easy-to-care-for plant, which makes it a great wedding favor. You can purchase succulents online in bulk from So Succulent (www.blossomfarm.com). You can even order the plants in small galvanized pails or miniature watering cans, ready for gifting. Include care instructions for guests, along with a thank-you tag.

## Seed Packet Favors

Seed packets make terrific wedding favors because they are useful and inexpensive. To create a unique favor, customize muslin drawstring bags with a floral stamp, and place a seed packet inside. Print a message on kraft tags, telling guests, "Love Has Bloomed," punch a hole in the tags, string twine through it, then tie it around the muslin bags. Secure it with a bow.

Or, design your own custom seed-packet favors. At www.EarthlyGoods.com, you can custom design the front and back of a seed packet to include your names and wedding date.

### Soap Favors

Soap is one favor you know guests will use. Place a handful of miniature soaps in a small spice bag (my favorite source for these is RegencyWraps.com) you've customized with a thank-you stamp. Look for unique soap shapes at www.soapsationalsoaps.etsy.com: cowboy boots for a Western wedding, Eiffel Tower soaps for a Parisian theme, starfish for a beach wedding, or sailboats for a nautical theme.

### Ornaments

If you're having a winter wedding, you can create ornament favors. Buy clear plastic, round ornaments, craft paint, and coordinating ribbon. Remove the metal ornament hook, pour a small amount of paint inside the ornament, and gently swirl the ornament to allow the paint to spread across the surface. Keep rotating until the color covers the entire surface; if needed, add more paint. Allow the paint to dry overnight by standing the ornaments upright in cupcake wrappers; once it's dry, reattach the metal hook and tie a ribbon loop to the hook for easy hanging.

Or purchase unfinished wood-frame ornaments at a craft store. Paint the wood using a sponge brush and craft paint; once it's dry, insert a photo of you and your fiancé, or a printed message that says thank you, or leave the frame empty for your guests to fill as they wish. A decorative ribbon finishes the piece.

### Matches

Give guests matchbox favors to symbolize how you and your spouse are "A Perfect Match." Places like www.ForYourParty.com allow you to order matchboxes in a wide range of patterns, colors, and sizes, and with custom text.

You can make your own match "box" favors using loose wooden matches, small glass jars (with a cork or plastic topper), kraft tags, a hole punch, and ribbon. Fill the jars with matches and close. Print your own "Perfect Match" tags and secure them to the jar by punching a hole in the side of the tags and threading a ribbon through it.

## Coasters

You can create unique fabric-covered coasters with 4-inch cork rounds (available in a bulk pack of about 24 for under $15 on Amazon.com). Use a pencil to trace the cork round on the back side of a piece of fabric and cut. Secure the fabric to one side of the cork round with a thin layer of hot glue; smooth the fabric with your fingers to eliminate any wrinkles. To waterproof, apply a layer of glue sealant (Mod Podge works great) with a sponge brush over the fabric; when it's dry, apply a second coat.

Feeling artistic? If you have pretty penmanship, use a gold or silver metallic paint pen to draw, write, or stencil a design on top of a cork coaster. To prevent the design from fading, coat the top with a few layers of a glue sealant. Tie four coasters together in a set with ribbon.

You can also make coaster favors using inexpensive ceramic tiles (4¼ inches square) found at home-supply stores. Buy enough tiles to gift four coasters per person. Cut patterned scrapbook paper to fit the top of the tile surface; apply glue to the tile using a sponge brush. Attach the paper, using your fingers to smooth out any wrinkles. Apply a coat of glue sealant over the paper; when it's dry, apply another coat. Attach two adhesive felt dots (look for these at a hardware or home-supply store) to the bottom of each tile (to protect table surfaces). Tie each set of four coasters together with twine or ribbon.

Or, create a set of decorative coaster favors using ceramic tiles, acrylic paint, stencils, a sponge brush, clear sealant, and adhesive felt dots. Paint the tops of the ceramic tiles and let them dry, then set a stencil on top and apply another color with a sponge brush. Wait until they're dry, then apply a second coat. Finish each with a clear coat of sealant. Place two adhesive felt dots on the bottom of each tile.

## Lanterns

For a favor that doubles as outdoor décor, consider creating Mason jar lanterns. Use them to add a romantic glow to your reception site or to light pathways to the parking lot or restroom area. After the last song is played, announce to guests that the lanterns may be taken home as favors.

Use one-quart Mason jars. Wrap wire around the mouth of each one to create a sturdy handle, adding beading for a decorative touch, if you like. Fill each jar one-third full with clean sand and snug a votive down into it, then tie a thank-you tag around the top. If you'd like to be able to hang the lanterns inside a tent (or you want to be extra careful), don't bother with the sand, and instead set a battery-operated candle in each jar.

## Plant a Tree

Instead of a take-home favor, give back to nature and plant trees in your guests' honor. Create a note for each guest on card stock, thanking him or her for attending your wedding and sharing the news of the tree being planted in his or her honor.

## A Donation

In lieu of spending your budgeted money on favors, why not contribute to a cause about which you are passionate? For instance, if you are an animal lover, consider a donation to a local animal shelter. Or, if you are inspired by music, contribute money to a local children's-music program toward purchasing sheet music, instruments, or supplies to keep music playing in your town.

If you can't donate money, an equally valuable donation is your time. Volunteer at a children's hospital to teach a craft, read a book, or sing a song. Or volunteer to plant trees or flowers in your community park. If you decide to donate money or time, print the details on card stock to share with your guests — help you'll be helping to promote their awareness of a particular charity.

# Afterwords

*This book has come to an end, but your story is just beginning.*
*Long after the cake is cut, the last song is played, and you're whisked away on your*
*honeymoon, the memories of planning your beautifully handcrafted wedding will live on.*

*Enjoy every minute of it.*

*—E.*

# Index

Page numbers in *italic* indicate DIY projects with detailed instructions.

# Credits

The Publisher wishes to thank the following for permission to reproduce images and projects.

**Abbreviation key:** ur, upper right; mr, middle right; lr, lower right; ll, lower left; ml, middle left; ul, upper left. All credits are noted clockwise from the top right.

**Cover photography credits:**
*Front cover, center:* © 2012 AKaiser/Shutterstock, © 2012 LittleRambo/Shutterstock, © Texturis/Shutterstock, ur © 2012 Michelle Gardella Photography www.michellegardella.com with Everthine Bridal Boutique www.shopeverthine.com, lr © 2012 Eric Boneske Photography www.ericboneskephotography.com, ll © 2012 Eric Boneske Photography, ml © 2012 Eric Boneske Photography, ul © 2012 Michelle Gardella Photography.
*Back cover, center:* © 2012 LittleRambo/Shutterstock, ur © 2012 Carolyn Scott Photography www.carolynscottphotography.com, ul © 2012 Thomas Gardella for Michelle Gardella Photography.
*Center Back flap, author photograph:* © 2012 Revelry Photography www.revelryphotos.com, © 2012 Triff/Shutterstock.

**Interior photography credits:**
**p. 2** © 2012 Akimbo Design www.akimbo.com.au. **p. 4** © 2012 Samm Blake www.sammblake.com, © 2012 LittleRambo/Shutterstock. **p. 6** lr © 2012 Samm Blake, ll © 2012 Michelle Gardella Photography, © 2012 LittleRambo/Shutterstock. **p. 7** lr © 2012 Michelle Gardella Photography with Everthine Bridal Boutique, ll © 2012 Michelle Gardella Photography, ul © 2012 Thomas Gardella for Michelle Gardella Photography. **p. 8** © 2012 Susan Pacek Photography www.susanpacekphotography.com. **p. 10** © 2012 Carolyn Scott Photography. **p. 11** © 2012 LittleRambo/Shutterstock. **p. 12** © 2012 LittleRambo/Shutterstock, © 2012 Diana Elizabeth Photography www.dianaelizabeth.com. **p. 13** © 2012 Thomas Gardella for Michelle Gardella Photography. **p. 14** © 2012 Eric Boneske Photography. **p. 16** Thomas Gardella for Michelle Gardella Photography. **p. 17** © 2012 Carolyn Scott Photography. **p. 18** © 2012 Night Owl Paper Goods www.nightowlpapergoods.com. **p. 19** ur © 2012 Carolyn Scott Photography, lr © 2012 Akimbo Design. **p. 20** © 2012 Akimbo Design. **p. 22** © 2012 Michelle Gardella Photography. **p. 23** © 2012 Paper and Thread www.paperandthread.com. **p. 24** © 2012 Akimbo Design. **p. 25** © 2012 Carolyn Scott Photography. **p. 26** © 2012 Eric Boneske Photography, dress by Claire LaFaye www.clairelafaye.com, courtesy of Governor Thomas Bennett House www.governorthomasbennetthouse.com. **p. 28** © 2012 Michelle Gardella Photography with Everthine Bridal Boutique. **p. 29** lr © 2012 One Tree Photo+Cinema www.onetreephotography.com, ul © 2012 Michelle Gardella Photography. **p. 30** lr © 2012 Michelle Gardella Photography with Everthine Bridal Boutique, ul © 2012 Michelle Gardella Photography. **p. 31** © 2012 Michelle Gardella Photography. **p. 32** © 2012 Michelle Gardella Photography. **p. 33** lr © 2012 Thomas Gardella for Michelle Gardella Photography, ul © 2012 Michelle Gardella Photography. **p. 34** © 2012 Michelle Gardella Photography. **p. 35** ur © 2012 Michelle Gardella Photography, lr © 2012 Eric Boneske Photography. **p. 36** ur © 2012 Michelle Gardella Photography, ll © 2012 Carolyn Scott Photography, ul © 2012 Michelle Gardella Photography. **p. 37** © 2012 Michelle Gardella Photography. **p. 38** © 2012 Eric Boneske Photography. **p. 39** © 2012 Revelry Photography. **p. 40** © 2012 Eric Boneske Photography. **p. 41** ur © 2012 Michelle Gardella Photography, lr © 2012 Michelle Gardella Photography, jewelry by Lon Koosh www.lonkoosh.etsy.com, ul © 2012 Michelle Gardella Photography. **p. 42** © 2012 Eric Boneske Photography. **p. 43** © 2012 Eric Boneske Photography. **p. 44** © 2012 Revelry Photography. **p. 45** © 2012 Acres of Hope Photography www.acresofhopephotography.com. **p. 46** ur © 2012 Thomas Gardella for Michelle Gardella Photography, lr © 2012 Michelle Gardella Photography. **p. 47** © 2012 Aric and Casey Photography www.aricandcasey.com, bouquet and boutonniere by Eden's Echo www.edensecho. com. **p. 48** © 2012 Thomas Gardella for Michelle Gardella Photography. **p. 49** © 2012 Michelle Gardella

# Acknowledgments

I'd like to thank the team at Sellers Publishing, Inc., especially Robin Haywood and Charlotte Cromwell, who offered their expertise and brought this book to fruition. A big thank you to Marilyn Allen, of Allen O'Shea Literary Agency, who took me under her wing and lead me to this opportunity. I'm truly blessed! Thank you to my editor, Pam Hoenig, for offering her guidance. Thank you to Christine Dwyer for paying it forward. This book wouldn't have come to life without beautiful imagery to accompany the text, so I'd like to give a huge outpouring of gratitude to photographers who contributed their work especially Michelle Gardella, Thomas Gardella, Tania Sones, Megan LaBarbera, Eric Boneske, Carolyn Scott, Susan Pacek, Samm Blake, Diana Elizabeth, Matt Frye, Erica Schneider, Aric and Casey Lampert, Caroline Tran, Kama Demczyk, and Joey Kennedy. A huge high five and a thank you goes to photographer Andrew Arendoski of Revelry Photography who assisted with the many DIY projects and additional photographs for this book. I appreciate it so much. Last but not least, I'd like to thank handmade artisans everywhere for inspiring this book: you make the world a more beautiful place.

–Emma Arendoski
www.emmalinebride.com